# HEREFORDSHIRE CURIOSITIES

NIC HOWES has lived in Herefordshire for twelve years; he teaches Geography at a comprehensive school in the county. He regularly accompanies groups of children on educational visits to the countryside.

JANE CALOW is a visual artist, art historian and teacher; she has lived in the county for fourteen years. She exhibits her paintings and drawings locally and nationally.

33  St Catherine's Church, Hoarwithy

# HEREFORDSHIRE CURIOSITIES

Nic Howes

with drawings by
Jane Calow

ARCH

© Nic Howes 1990

Drawings © Jane Calow 1990

Published by ARCH, The Hope
Lyonshall, Nr. Kington, Herefordshire HR5 5HT

Cover photograph: Igg Welthy

Photoset in Mergenthaler Bembo and Centaur
at Five Seasons Press, Madley, Hereford

Printed and bound in Great Britain
by Billings and Sons Limited, Worcester

British Library Catologuing in Publication Data
Howes, Nic
Herefordshire curiosities
1. Curiosities
I. Title
030

ISBN 0 947618 05 8

# Contents

| | | |
|---|---|---|
| 1 | Aconbury *The Medicinal Waters of St Anne's Well* page | 11 |
| 2 | Ashperton *The Forgotten Canal Tunnel* | 12 |
| 3 | Aymestry *A Valley Eroded by a Torrent of Glacial Melt-Water* | 13 |
| 4 | Bacton *Monument to a Maid of Honour* | 14 |
| 5 | Brilley *Site of a House Cut by the Welsh Border* | 15 |
| 6 | Brinsop *Windows Commemorating William Wordsworth* | 17 |
| 7 | Brockhampton-by-Ross *A Thatched 'Arts and Crafts' Church* | 18 |
| 8 | Brockhampton-by-Ross *The Cathedral Quarry* | 19 |
| 9 | Burrington *Cast Iron Monuments* | 20 |
| 10 | Canon Pyon/King's Pyon *Robin Hood's Butts* | 21 |
| 11 | Clifford *An Obelisk Built by the Unemployed* | 22 |
| 12 | Colwall *The Swedish Nightingale's Last Home* | 23 |
| 13 | Colwall *Hope End—a Moorish Fantasy* | 24 |
| 14 | Craswall *A Ruined Grandmontine Priory* | 25 |
| 15 | Credenhill *Thomas Traherne's Church* | 26 |
| 16 | Cusop *Mouse Castle—Scene of a Curious Party* | 28 |
| 17 | Dinmore *Dinmore Manor—a Fantasy Come True* | 29 |
| 18 | Dinmore *A Swift One at the Spitfire* | 30 |
| 19 | Dorstone *The Ancient Oaks of Moccas Park* | 31 |
| 20 | Dorstone *Arthur's Stone—Remains of a Neolithic Burial Chamber* | 32 |
| 21 | Downton *A Marvel of the 'Picturesque'* | 33 |
| 22 | Eastnor *Obelisk in Memory of a Lost Son* | 34 |
| 23 | Eastnor *The Giant's Cave* | 35 |
| 24 | Eastnor *The Red Earl's Dyke* | 36 |
| 25 | Eastnor *The Curse of Raggedstone* | 37 |
| 26 | Fownhope *Memorial to a Champion Boxer* | 39 |
| 27 | Fownhope *Whipping Post and Stocks* | 40 |
| 28 | Foy *A Parish Held Together by a Footbridge* | 41 |
| 29 | Garway *An Ancient Dovecote and Unusual Church Remains* | 42 |
| 30 | Hampton Bishop *An Isolated Bridge over the River Lugg* | 43 |
| 31 | Hereford *The Twisted Spire* | 44 |
| 32 | Hereford *St Ethelbert's Well* | 45 |
| 33 | Hoarwithy *An Outstanding Italianate Church* | 46 |
| 34 | Hope Mansell *The Dancing Green* | 47 |
| 35 | Hope Mansell *The Spoil Heap from a Gold Mine* | 48 |
| 36 | Kentchurch *The Bridge where the Devil was Tricked* | 49 |
| 37 | Kilpeck *Famous Norman Carvings* | 50 |
| 38 | Kingsland *Site of the Battle of Mortimer's Cross* | 51 |
| 39 | Kington Rural *The Legend of the Whet Stone* | 52 |
| 40 | Kington Rural *The Black Dog of Hergest* | 53 |

| | | |
|---|---|---|
| 41 | Ledbury Rural *The Big Viaduct over a Small River* | 54 |
| 42 | Ledbury *Pride and Greed and some Relics of the Civil War* | 55 |
| 43 | Leominster *A Mobile Ducking Stool* | 56 |
| 44 | Letton *An 'Oxbow Lake'* | 57 |
| 45 | Little Birch *A Glastonbury Thorn* | 58 |
| 46 | Llangarron *A Remarkable 'Misfit' Stream* | 59 |
| 47 | Longtown *The Sad Story of the 'Longtown Harriers'* | 60 |
| 48 | Lucton *A Landscape of 'Drumlins'* | 61 |
| 49 | Lugwardine *Memorial to a Horse* | 62 |
| 50 | Mansell Lacy *The House with a Built-in Dovecote* | 63 |
| 51 | Mordiford *The Spot where a Dragon was Slain* | 64 |
| 52 | Much Dewchurch *Tram Inn* | 65 |
| 53 | Much Dewchurch *Visits from a Ghost Story Writer* | 66 |
| 54 | Much Marcle *'The Wonder'* | 67 |
| 55 | Much Marcle *The Tree You Can Sit Inside* | 68 |
| 56 | Pembridge *A Wooden Bell-House* | 69 |
| 57 | Peterchurch *The Fish with the Gold Chain* | 70 |
| 58 | Pipe and Lyde *The Centre of Herefordshire* | 71 |
| 59 | Ross-on-Wye *The Old Prison* | 72 |
| 60 | Ross-on-Wye *The Gazebo Tower* | 73 |
| 61 | Ross-on-Wye *The Banjo Player's Grave* | 74 |
| 62 | Saint Margarets *A Beautiful Carved Wooden Rood Screen* | 75 |
| 63 | Sellack *Obscure Suspension Footbridge over the River Wye* | 76 |
| 64 | Sellack *A Very Simple Epitaph* | 78 |
| 65 | Shobdon *The Unidentified Architect and the Norman Carvings* | 79 |
| 66 | Turnastone *An Unusual Enamel Sign* | 80 |
| 67 | Walford *The Valley without a River* | 81 |
| 68 | Walford *Relic of a Forgotten Brew* | 82 |
| 69 | Walterstone *The Abandoned Garden* | 83 |
| 70 | Welsh Bicknor *Monument to a Family Tragedy* | 84 |
| 71 | Welsh Newton *The Saint's Grave* | 85 |
| 72 | Whitbourne *A Vinegar Baron's Mansion* | 86 |
| 73 | Whitchurch *An Unusual Way to Cross the River* | 87 |
| 74 | Whitchurch *King Arthur's Cave* | 88 |
| 75 | Whitchurch *Seven Sisters Rocks* | 89 |
| 76 | Whitney-on-Wye *Wooden Toll Bridge* | 90 |
| 77 | Whitney-on-Wye *The Abandoned Footbridge* | 91 |
| 78 | Wigmore *Picturesque Ruin* | 92 |
| 79 | Wigmore *The Former Bed of a Large Ice-Age Lake* | 93 |
| 80 | Yarkhill *The Skew Bridge* | 94 |
| | *References* | 95 |

# Acknowledgements

I would like to acknowledge the contributions made to the compilation of this book by Mike Booth, Roger Calow, Michael Hudson, Revd Martin Reed, Colin Sanders, Martyn Urquhart, Hilary Ward, Bob Wreford, Gordon Wood and many other Herefordshire people who have made helpful suggestions. I must also thank the Fellows of Lady Margaret Hall, Oxford and finally my family, Jane and Asa.

The front cover photograph by Igg Welthy
shows one of Kilvert's *grey old men of Moccas*. See page 31.

The back cover illustration uses a photograph kindly supplied by Patricia Hegarty of Hope End Counrty Hotel.

# HEREFORDSHIRE

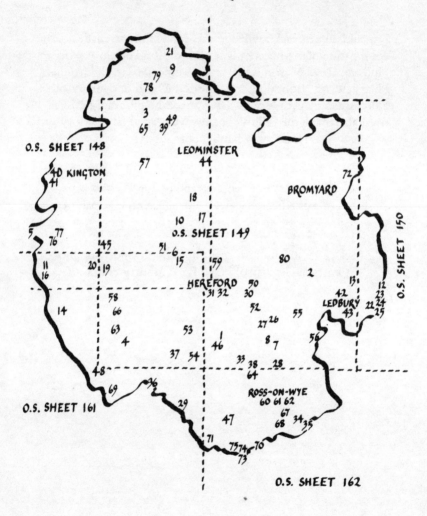

21
9
79
78

3
65  39 49

O.S. SHEET 148

40 KINGTON
41

LEOMINSTER
44

57

72

BROMYARD

18

10  17

O.S. SHEET 149

O.S. SHEET 150

5
76 77

45
51  6

15  59

80

2

13  12

11
16

20  19

HEREFORD  50
31 32  30

42  23
LEDBURY  22 24
43  25

58
66

52

27 26  55

56

14

63
4

53

1
46

8  7

37  54

33
38  28
64

48

69  36

29

ROSS-ON-WYE
60 61 62

O.S. SHEET 161

47

67
68  34
35

71

75 74  70
73

O.S. SHEET 162

# Introduction

I have tried to assemble a diverse collection of interesting places to visit, with the assumption that the would-be visitor will be using a car to travel in. Many of the curiosities are off the main tourist routes, and reaching some involves a short walk. The Ordnance Survey maps are therefore very useful.

The location map shows the area covered by each of the five relevant 1:50000 'Landranger' maps.

The curiosities are listed in alphabetical order of the parishes in which they lie. I hope you enjoy seeking them out amidst the beautiful countryside this county has to offer—good hunting!

9 *Cast Iron Monument, Burrington*

# 1 Aconbury
## The Medicinal Waters of St Anne's Well

Legend has it that the waters of St Anne's Well have healing properties. The first water to bubble up in this well after midnight on Twelfth Night was said to emit a blue smoke and to be of great medicinal value, especially for eye troubles.

₢The well can still be identified today as a spring around which a small retaining wall has been built. Although it is sadly delapidated, water still emerges in its immediate vicinity to feed a small stream. The well is in a very secluded spot, and it is easy to forget you are close to the bustle of Hereford and the traffic on the main road.

POSITION: In a hollow on the north-east facing slope of Aconbury Hill, which is a prominent summit to the east of the A49 Hereford to Ross-on-Wye road.

▷ Ordnance Map (1:50000). Hereford and Leominster 149.
▷ Ordnance Map (1:25000). Hereford (South). Pathfinder 1040 (SO 43/53).
MAP REFERENCE: 512334.

ACCESS: Take the minor left turn signposted to Aconbury from the top of Callow hill on the A49 out of Hereford towards Ross. About a mile and a half down this lane, by a sharp left-hand bend (Map Reference 514334), a public right of way leads off to the right, up across the fields and into the woods which cover the top of Aconbury Hill. Follow this path for about 300 metres and St Anne's well is then about 150 metres to your right, just beyond the field boundary (off the right of way).

# 2 Ashperton
## *The Forgotten Canal Tunnel*

Ashperton canal tunnel is one of the obscure remnants of the unsuccessful Hereford and Gloucester canal (also see Yarkhill). The construction of the tunnel severely taxed the abilities of the canal's talented engineer, Stephen Ballard (1804-1891). Whilst planning the route of the canal in 1838, Ballard decided to opt for a short tunnel (400 yards) with long and deep approach cuttings. Work began on the tunnel and cuttings in 1841; explosives were necessary, but some good stone was removed for construction purposes. For more than a year, Ballard lived near the tunnel in a temporary home built largely of dry bricks, coping with problems including flooding of the shafts and landslides in the approach cuttings. The tunnel was eventually completed in 1842.

¶The most obvious and accessible evidence of the tunnel is the curious line of grassy mounds which links the two portals above ground. These mounds are 'spoil' from the tunnel excavations. Nearby is the delightful Canon Frome and District bowling green. Also worth visiting is the recently restored Tunnel House, by the edge of the cutting at the east end of the tunnel. The tunnel portals are both very difficult to reach, and are on private land. There is footpath access to some of the bridges across the cuttings, both of which still contain water.

POSITION: Just east of Ashperton village.
▷ Ordnance Map (1:50000). Hereford and Leominster 149.
▷ Ordnance Map (1:25000). Great Malvern. Pathfinder 1018 (SO 64/74).
MAP REFERENCES: Western portal: 649420. Eastern portal and Tunnel House: 653418.

ACCESS: Take the A4103 Worcester road out of Hereford and turn right at Newtown (about 9 miles out) onto the A417. 3 miles down this road turn left opposite Ashperton school. In about half a mile you reach a right-hand bend, where a gate leads to the bowling green. If you continue along the lane for a few hundred metres you reach a parking space on the left, just before Tunnel House. The footpath from this point back to the bowling green follows the line of mounds produced by the tunnelling.

# 3 Aymestry

## A Valley Eroded by a Torrent of Glacial Melt-Water

Strange though it may seem today, Herefordshire once had an Arctic climate, and much of the county was covered by ice. The last ice advance into Herefordshire is estimated to have occurred about 20,000 years ago. At this time there were long, broad tongues of ice stretching out from the Welsh hills into the Herefordshire lowlands.

¶ One such tongue made its way north-east along the foot of the hills around Aymestry to stop at the village of Orleton. The presence of the ice created a barrier to streams flowing south from Aymestry, and several lakes began to 'pond up' amongst the hills. One of these lakes developed as a consequence of an ice dam at Covenhope (map reference 408642). Eventually the rising water level in this lake reached a notch point in the surrounding hills, through which it could escape. The rush of escaping water cut a deep gorge now referred to as the Sned Wood channel. The depth and straightness of the channel suggest that it was guided by a fault (a break in the rocks, often creating a straight line of weakness). Looking along the gorge from the Lye road, one cannot fail to be impressed by the scale of the valley and the forces which formed it.

POSITION: A mile to the west of the A4110 Hereford to Knighton road at Aymestry.
▷ Ordnance Map (1:50000). Hereford and Leominster 149.
▷ Ordnance Map (1:25000). Tenbury Wells and Mortimers Cross. Pathfinder 972 (SO 46/56).
MAP REFERENCE: Grid Square 4065.

ACCESS: Approaching from Hereford, cross the River Lugg by the Crown public house in Aymestry and take the first left turn (which leads to Lingen and Lye). The valley is best viewed in cross-section from a point about half a mile along this road (map reference 417662).

# 4 Bacton

## Monument to a Maid of Honour

Blanche Parry was a maid of honour of Queen Elizabeth I. Her monument in Bacton church provides a surprising link between the famous monarch and a remote parish in the foothills of the Black Mountains. The monument itself is also very curious. This is because of the relative sizes and positions of the figures of Blanche and the Queen. The two figures are similar in size, but Blanche is kneeling in profile whilst the Queen is facing forward in an awkward posture—a secular version of the medieval motif of the worshipper kneeling before the Virgin. There is a long inscription with Elizabethan spelling which demands careful deciphering. Although not a highly skilled piece of workmanship, the monument is well worth seeking out.

POSITION: In Bacton church. Ordnance Map (1:50000). Hereford and Leominster 149.
▷ Ordnance Map (1:25000). Golden Valley. Pathfinder 1039 (SO 23/33).
MAP REFERENCE: 371323.
ACCESS: Turn left off the B4347 Pontrilas to Vowchurch road at a sharp right hand bend about one mile beyond Abbey Dore. Bacton church is less than half a mile up this lane. There is a small car park by the churchyard gate—turn left off the lane mentioned above. The church is usually unlocked.

# 5 Brilley
## Site of a House Cut by the Welsh Border

An interesting curiosity is referred to by Francis Kilvert (see entry for Cusop) in his diary for Friday 18th November, 1870. Whilst visiting Mrs Powell at a cottage called 'The Pant' he became engaged in conversation about parish boundaries:

> I'm sitting in Brilley (England and Herefordshire) now,' said I, feeling for the boundary notch in the chimney. 'It's further this way,' she said. 'I suppose,' she said, 'there have been some curious disputes about the boundary running through this house.' 'Very odd indeed,' I said, remembering the extraordinary story which old Betty Williams of Crowther used to tell me about the birth of a child in this house (the Pant) and the care taken that the child should be born in England in the English corner of the cottage. 'Stand here, Betsey, in this corner,' said the midwife. And the girl was delivered of the child STANDING.

¶The isolated site of 'The Pant', which fortunately lies beside a public right of way, is identifiable as the remains of a dwelling with a small area of land enclosed around it. The house appears abandoned as early as 1887, when the Ordnance Survey was first carried out.

¶It is also worth noting that in several places in Brilley parish, the border runs up the middle of the road!

POSITION: Near Crowther's Pool, in the far west of Brilley parish.
▷ Ordnance Map (1:50000). Presteigne and Hay-on-Wye 148.
▷ Ordnance Map (1:25000). Hay-on-Wye. Pathfinder 1016 (SO 24/ 34).
MAP REFERENCE: 222478.
ACCESS: Turn off the A438 Hereford to Brecon road at Rhydspence and drive past the Inn and up the steep right-hand bend beyond. Fork right after about a mile and then continue for a further mile, stopping just after you have crossed the stream (the Wales/England border) for a second time. You will almost certainly need the Pathfinder map to follow the footpath south-east across two fields to reach the site of 'The Pant'.

# ROMAN ANTIQUITIES DISCOVERED
## AT
# BISHOPSTONE, HEREFORDSHIRE

*(published 1835)*

*While poring Antiquarians search the ground*
*Upturned with curious pains, the Bard, a Seer,*
*Takes fire:— The men that have been reappear;*
*Romans for travel girt, for business gowned;*
*And some recline on couches, myrtle-crowned,*
*In festal glee: why not? For fresh and clear,*
*As if its hues were of the passing year,*
*Dawns this time-buried pavement. From that mound*
*Hoards may come forth of Trojans, Maximins,*
*Shrunk into coins with all their warlike toil:*
*Or a fierce impress issues with its foil*
*Of tenderness—the Wolf, whose suckling Twins*
*The unlettered ploughboy pities when he wins*
*The casual treasure from the furrowed soil.*

William Wordsworth

# 6 Brinsop

## Stained Glass Windows Commemorating William Wordsworth

William Wordsworth, the famous poet, occasionally stayed with his brother-in-law at Brinsop Court (map reference 446458), itself an interesting building, but not open to the public. In 1835, at the age of 65, he came to visit and is thought to have written some sonnets whilst in the area. It is likely that the lines opposite were written at this time.

❡Brinsop's neighbouring parishes of Bishopstone and Kenchester contain Roman remains including a road and a town (the latter is centred on map reference 441428). The local excitement at their discovery understandably fired the poet's imagination.

❡The stained glass window in memory of Wordsworth is in the chancel. There is also a window in the Lady chapel in memory of Dorothy (his sister), Mary (his wife) and Dorothy (his daughter). The twelfth century 'Herefordshire School' stone carvings also repay inspection.

POSITION: Brinsop church.
▷ Ordnance Map (1:50000). Hereford and Leominster 149.
▷ Ordnance Map (1:25000). Hereford (North). Pathfinder 1017 (SO 44/54).
MAP REFERENCE: 442448.
ACCESS: Turn right off the A480 Hereford to Kington road one mile beyond the R.A.F. camp at Credenhill. Turn right off this lane after about 500 metres and follow the very minor road amongst various buildings to a small car-park by the churchyard gate.

# 7 Brockhampton-by-Ross
## A Thatched 'Arts and Crafts' Church

This very attractive thatched church is by W. R. Lethaby, 1901-2, who was part of the 'Arts and Crafts' movement led by William Morris. The beauty of Brockhampton is that it is not merely a copy of a medieval church; it is an original design, medieval in spirit but not afraid to make use of early twentieth century materials. Inside, for example, one finds dramatic stone arches supporting concrete vaulting. Another special feature is the tapestry designed by Burne-Jones and made by Morris and Co., depicting two angels.
℄ The church has been described as one of the most convincing and impressive of its date in any country and is well worth a visit.

POSITION: Brockhampton-by-Ross.
▷ Ordnance Map (1:50000). Hereford and Leominster 149.
▷ Ordnance Map (1:25000). Hereford (South). Pathfinder 1040 (SO 43/53).
MAP REFERENCE: 594321.

ACCESS: Turn right off the B4224 Hereford to Ross-on-Wye road at Fownhope church. After the steep, wooded ascent of Capler Hill, turn left at the cross-roads and Brockhampton church is 300 metres on the left. Travelling from Ross, it is simpler to turn left off the B4224 at Gurney's Oak pub. This lane brings you straight to Brockhampton church.

# 8 Brockhampton-by-Ross
## *The Cathedral Quarry*

This large quarry is reputed to be the source of the stone used to build Hereford Cathedral in the Middle Ages. The River Wye would have provided a convenient transport route. On the river-bank below the quarry are the remains of stonework that might have once been a quay of some kind.

POSITION: On the steep west flank of Capler Hill, overlooking the River Wye.
▷ Ordnance Map (1:50000). Hereford and Leominster 149.
▷ Ordnance Map (1:25000). Hereford (South). Pathfinder 1040 (SO 43/53).
MAP REFERENCE: 589324.

ACCESS: Take the Capler/Brockhampton lane which leads out of Fownhope next to the church. After about a mile, just beyond Capler Cottages, a public right of way leads off on the right (map reference 587328). Follow this right of way southwards, down-stream along the Wye for about 500 metres and the quarry is up in the woods on your left; a track leads off towards it opposite a cor-rugated iron hut. If you go further along the right of way you reach a cobbled section, and just beyond this are the 'quay' remains.

N.B. This land is part of the Brockhampton Estate and is also a Site of Special Scientific Interest.

# 9 Burrington
## Cast Iron Monuments

Outside the east wall of the church is a row of six large cast-iron tombstones dated 1619–1754. These are monuments to members of the Knight family, who had interests in the iron making industry in Shropshire. This is probably the reason for the choice of this rather unusual material for their monuments. Note that the tombstones include that of the famous ironmaster, Richard Knight (1659–1745), who moved to this area from Shropshire in 1685; he set up a forge at Bringewood (near Forge Bridge—see Downton).

POSITION: Burrington church lies about three miles from Leintwardine along a minor road to the south-east.
▷ Ordnance Map (1:50000). Presteigne and Hay-on-Wye 148.
▷ Ordnance Map (1:25000). Ludlow. Pathfinder 951 (SO 47/57).
MAP REFERENCE: 442721.

ACCESS: Take the A4110 Hereford to Leintwardine (and Knighton) road and turn right immediately after crossing the Teme bridge in Leintwardine. Follow the signposts to Burrington (about three miles).

# 10  Canon Pyon/King's Pyon
## *Robin Hood's Butts*

The odd conical shape of these two hills has long exercised popular imagination. Most legends involve the dropping of loose earth by supernatural beings. In one account Robin Hood and Little John set out with spades of earth to destroy the monks at Wormsley (a mile or so south-west). On the way they meet a cobbler and ask him how far it is to Wormsley. Sensing evil afoot, the cobbler tells them that they would wear out all the boots he has for sale long before they reached their destination. At this the two travellers give up their mission and drop their spadefuls, thus forming the two hills.

¶The less exciting explanation of the hills is that they are made up of harder rock than that worn away by tributaries of the River Lugg.

POSITION: To the left of the A4110 Hereford to Knighton road at Canon Pyon.
▷Ordnance Map (1:50000) Hereford and Leominster 149.
▷Ordnance Map (1:25000) Hereford (North). Pathfinder 1017 (SO 44/54).

MAP REFERENCES: 455495 and 439491 (summits).

ACCESS: There are no public rights of way onto the hills themselves, but there is a network of roads and paths around them. The distinctive shape of the hills makes them recognisable from many points in the county. They are clearly visible from the main road through Canon Pyon.

# 11 Clifford
## An Obelisk Built by the Unemployed

The remnants of The Moor Mansion and its associated estate lie in this far-flung corner of the county. On a hillside overlooking the estate stands an obelisk built to the order of Anna Maria Broadbelt Stallard-Penoyre, who succeeded to the estate in January 1827. The work is thought to have been carried out to relieve unemployment.

POSITION: To the south of the B4348 Golden Valley to Hay-on-Wye road, one mile before the town of Hay.
▷ Ordnance Map (1:50000). Abergavenny and the Black Mountains 161.
▷ Ordnance Map (1:25000). Hay-on-Wye. Pathfinder 1016 (SO 24/34).
MAP REFERENCE: 247429.

ACCESS: The obelisk is visible from the road described above; you should look close to the edge of Mouse Castle Wood, next to a tree.

# 12 Colwall
## *The Swedish Nightingale's Last Home*

Jenny Lind (1820–1887) was born in Sweden, unwanted, illegitimate and unloved. She became an internationally famous, much adored and idolised singer, often referred to as the Swedish Nightingale. The degree of her popularity can be gauged by the fact that she was the first woman ever to be memorialised in Westminster Abbey, with a plaque in Poet's Corner.

¶In 1877 her daughter married into a Herefordshire family, and it was not long before Jenny and her husband, Otto, neither of whom were in good health, moved to the county. They bought two cottages and turned them into one house, reminiscent of a Swiss chalet, which they named 'Wynd's Point'. To surprise Otto, she had a small rustic arbour built in a Swedish style. Jenny loved the woods, meadows and wild birds of the area, and appreciated the importance of the local geology: 'The oldest rocks the earth can boast are in my little garden'.

¶Her last public performance was given at the Malvern Hills Spa for the Railway Servant's Benevolent Fund. Local legend has it that the applause was so tumultuous that it split the roof open.

POSITION: At the crest of the Malvern Hills on the A449 Ledbury to Great Malvern road.
▷ Ordnance Map (1:50000). Worcester and The Malverns 150.
▷ Ordnance Map (1:25000). Great Malvern. Pathfinder 1018 (SO 64/74).
MAP REFERENCE: 765403.

ACCESS: Wynd's Point is only open on specific days in summer under the National Gardens Scheme (see the *Yellow Book* published each year by the N.G.S.). The drive to the house is on the left just beyond the British Camp Hotel on the A449 Ledbury to Great Malvern road. Access to the surrounding Malvern Hills is always open, and there are large car parks opposite the British Camp Hotel and behind it, a short distance up the B4232 road to Upper Colwall.

# 13 Colwall
## *Hope End — A Moorish Fantasy*

Hope End has at least two major claims to historical importance: it is a very early example of the Indo-Mooresque style in England, and was also the childhood home of Elizabeth Barrett-Browning. ⟨The house was built 1810–1815 for Edward Moulton-Barrett, who said, '. . . if I thought that there were another such (house) in England I would pull it down.' Although the Brighton Pavilion and Sezincote (Gloucestershire) were not far behind Hope End, it remained set apart because of its distinctive style. The house itself was demolished in 1867, but the remarkable stable block remains, and has been turned into a small Country Hotel (telephone 0531 3613). The stableyard wall is ornamented with oriental-style columns, and near the stable block is a minaret topped with a crescent. There is also a Moorish gateway-cum-clocktower.

POSITION: In the hills two miles north of Ledbury.
▷Ordnance Map (1:50000). Hereford and Leominster 149.
▷Ordnance Map (1:25000). Great Malvern. Pathfinder 1018 (SO 64/74).
MAP REFERENCE: 723412.

ACCESS: Take the Bromyard road north out of Ledbury; shortly after passing beneath the railway bridge on the edge of the town turn right to Wellington Heath. After passing through this settlement (one mile) you should bear right to reach the drive to Hope End; the Ordnance Map will greatly assist in finding the place.

# 14 Craswall
## A Ruined Grandmontine Priory

The Order of Grandmont was founded by Stephen of Muret in about 1100 near Limoges in France. His order was strictly contemplative. A ruthless simplicity of life was coupled with an unusually high degree of involvement of the lay brethren in administration, leaving the choir monks free to devote themselves to spiritual duties.

❡There were only three Houses of Grandmont ever established in England; Grosmont on the North York Moors in about 1204, and shortly afterwards Alderbury on the River Severn. Craswall was founded by Walter de Lacy, Sheriff of Herefordshire and Lord of Ewyas Harold, around 1225.

❡The wars between England and France from 1295 until 1413 led to Craswall and many other monasteries being classified as 'Alien Priories' and seized. Craswall lasted out until the reign of Henry VI, when it was granted to Christ's College, Cambridge, and the buildings were left to fall into ruin.

❡There are remains of dams and their associated fishponds to the south-east of the Priory. They can be reached along a public right of way from Abbey Farm.

POSITION: High up at the head of a remote valley in the Black Mountains four miles south-east of Hay-on-Wye.

▷ Ordnance Map (1:50000). Abergavenny and the Black Mountains 161.

▷ Ordnance Map (1:25000). Golden Valley. Pathfinder 1016 (SO 23/33).

MAP REFERENCE: 273376.

ACCESS: Craswall lies on the road from Hay-on-Wye to Longtown and will be very difficult to find without the 1:50000 Ordnance Survey map. You should aim for the highest point on the road (1450 feet), near which a track descends to the Priory ruins and Abbey Farm. The approach from Hay is fairly direct, whilst that from Hereford is best made via Clehonger, Kingstone, Vowchurch, Turnastone, and Michaelchurch Escley. It is courteous not to drive down the track, and a short walk brings you to a stream crossing with the Priory ruins accessible through a gate on your right.

[25]

# 15 Credenhill
## *Thomas Traherne's Church*

Credenhill's church of St Mary can have changed little since the time when the mystic, poet and writer Thomas Traherne was Rector here, from 1661 to 1667.

℄Traherne has been described as a man who became one of the most infectiously happy mortals this earth has ever known. He was born a shoemaker's son of Hereford around 1638. At the age of just fifteen he entered Brasenose College, Oxford.

℄Having been appointed to the living of Credenhill, Traherne returned to Herefordshire and took up his duties. A contemporary says of him: 'He was so wonderfully transported with the love of God . . . that those who would converse with him were forced to endure some discourse upon these subjects, whether they had any sense of Religion or not.'

℄Whilst at Credenhill he is believed to have written the *Meditations on the Six Days of the Creation* and *Meditations and Devotions upon the life of Christ*; he also began his *Centuries of Meditation*.

POSITION: About four and a half miles north-west of Hereford.
▷Ordnance Map (1:50000). Hereford and Leominster 149.
▷Ordnance Map (1:25000). Hereford (North). Pathfinder 1017 (SO 44/54).
MAP REFERENCE: 450439.

ACCESS: Take the A438 road out of Hereford towards Brecon. Turn right just after Wyevale garden centre onto the A480 towards Kington. Look out for a right turn up to Credenhill church, after you have passed the RAF base on your left.

The Sun, that gilded all the bordering Woods,
Shone from the sky
To beautify
My Earthly and my Hevenly Goods;
Exalted in his Throne on high,
He shed his Beams
In Golden Streams
That did illustrat all the sky;
Those Floods of Light, his mantle Rays,
Did fill the glittr'ing Ways,
While that unsufferable piercing Ey
The Ground did glorify.
The choicest Colors, Yellow, Green and Blew
Did all this Court
In comly sort
With mixt varieties bestrew;
Like Gold with Emeralds between;
As if my God
From his Abode
By these intended to be seen.
And so He was.

From the Preface to *The Contemplation* by Thomas Traherne,
a little book of *Thanksgivings* thought to have been written
at Credenhill.

## 16 Cusop
### Mouse Castle — Scene of a Curious Party

Mouse Castle itself is the remains of a Motte and Bailey castle. The diarist Francis Kilvert (1840–1879), curate at Clyro from 1865 to 1872 and later vicar of Bredwardine, recorded his thoughts about a curious group he observed on Mouse Castle. He describes watching a 'wild party' of children playing with a man they called 'father':

> *They were perfectly nondescript, seemed to have come from nowhere and be going nowhere, but just to have fallen from the sky upon Mouse Castle, and to be just amusing themseves . . . They were like no one whom I ever saw before.*

POSITION: On a wooded hilltop overlooking the town of Hay-on-Wye.
▷ Ordnance Map (1:50000). Presteigne and Hay-on-Wye 148.
▷ Ordnance Map (1:25000). Hay-on-Wye. Pathfinder 1016 (SO 24/ 34).
MAP REFERENCE: 248424.

ACCESS: Take the B4348 Dorstone/Bredwardine road out of Hay and about half a mile beyond the edge of the town take a right turn towards Michaelchurch Escley and Longtown. After about 400 metres along this road a footpath leads off on the left, opposite Lidiart-y-wain (named Lldyadyway on the latest 1:25000 map). The footpath crosses the field and enters Mouse Castle Wood at which point it swings right and then left to emerge on a minor lane along which you turn left to reach Mouse Castle (the total distance is about three quarters of a mile). The route from Lydiart-y-wain is the same as that described by Francis Kilvert in his diary, right down to the wood anemones if you go in the spring. Those who do not wish to walk this far should continue along the Longtown road beyond Lydiart-y-wain, uphill for just under a mile before turning left along the minor lane mentioned above (the turning is just before another fork in the road).

# 17 Dinmore

## Dinmore Manor — A Fantasy Come True

The Dinmore estate was purchased in 1927 by Richard Hollins Murray, the inventor of cats' eyes—three years after he had patented his invention. In the early 1930s the new owner made major alterations to the Manor House, including the addition of a remarkable Music Room and Cloisters, the latter built in the style of the fourteenth century. This interesting architectural flight of fancy is enhanced by its dramatic location on an elevated site. The cloisters overlook a rock garden which contains a Grotto.

¶ In the distant past the site was an important Commandery of the Knights Hospitaller of St John of Jerusalem.

¶ An informative illustrated booklet on the Manor, written by the late Richard Hollins Murray, is on sale to visitors.

POSITION: On high ground to the west of the A49 Hereford to Leominster road, north of Wellington.
▷ Ordnance Map (1:50000). Hereford and Leominster 149.
▷ Ordnance Map (1:25000). Leominster. Pathfinder 994 (SO 45/55).
MAP REFERENCE: 485504.

ACCESS: The drive to the house is signposted from the A49 Hereford to Leominster road, about five miles from Hereford. Parts of the house (including the Music Room and Cloisters) are open to visitors during much of the year. Opening times are shown at the roadside.

## 18 Dinmore

### A Swift One at the Spitfire

Looking out over the fields, woods and orchards of central Herefordshire stands a Supermarine Swift jet fighter aircraft, dating from about 1952. It has been a local landmark for over twenty years, since it was acquired by Sheppard's Surplus stores. Sheppard's carry a wide range of government surplus goods, including some curious pieces of military hardware. The building to the right of the large storehouse was originally the Red Lion public house. Its name was changed to the Spitfire when the firm acquired one of these famous aircraft, which also stood on the forecourt for many years. The pub was closed in the mid 1970s and the Spitfire is now in Canada.

POSITION: On the forecourt of Sheppard's Surplus stores at Upper Hill.
▷ Ordnance Map (1:50000). Hereford and Leominster 149.
▷ Ordnance Map (1:25000). Leominster. Pathfinder 994 (SO 45/55).
MAP REFERENCE: 472535.

ACCESS: Take the A4110 Hereford to Leintwardine (and Knighton) road to Bush Bank (about nine miles from Hereford) where you should turn right to Upper Hill. After about two miles you will reach Sheppard's Surplus stores on the right hand side of the road.

# 19 Dorstone
## The Ancient Oaks of Moccas Park

Moccas Park is an ancient deer park lying on the flanks of Dorstone Hill, overlooking the Wye valley. The park is one of the finest examples of wood pasture remaining in Britain, ranking in importance alongside the New Forest, Windsor Great Park and Sherwood Forest. The predominant parkland trees are oaks, some of which are very old. The park has been designated as a Site of Special Scientific Interest.

⟨Kilvert's Diary (22nd April, 1876) refers to the 'King Oak' of Moccas Park, which he said may have been 2,000 years old and which measured roughly 33 feet in girth. Kilvert goes on:

*I fear those grey old men of Moccas, those grey, gnarled, low browed, knock kneed, bowed, bent, huge, strange, long-armed, deformed, hunchbacked, misshapen oak men that stand waiting and watching century after century, biding God's time with both feet in the grave and yet tiring down and seeing out generation after generation, with such tales to tell, as when they whisper them to each other in the midsummer nights, make the silver birches weep and the poplars and aspens shiver and the long ears of the hares and rabbits stand on end. No human hand set these oaks. They are 'the trees which the Lord hath planted'. They look as if they had been at the beginning and making of the world, and they will probably see its end.*

POSITION: To the left of the B4352 Madley to Hay-on-Wye road between Blakemere and Bredwardine.
▷Ordnance Map (1:50000). Hereford and Leominster 149.
▷Ordnance Map (1:25000). Hay-on-Wye. Pathfinder 1016 (SO 24/34).
MAP REFERENCE: Grid squares 3342 and 3442.

ACCESS: There is no public access to Moccas Park, but there are excellent views of the many ancient oak trees as you travel along the B4352 Madley to Hay-on-Wye road between Blakemere and Bredwardine (about twelve miles from Hereford). For drivers it is best to park and walk along the road by the park boundary.

[31]

## 20 Dorstone

### Arthur's Stone — Remains of a Neolithic Burial Chamber

The remains consist of a chamber formed by vertical side slabs of stone supporting a single enormous capstone, estimated to weigh 25 tons. The construction of the tomb must have demanded a large labour force and a great deal of ingenuity, since only stone tools have been found during excavations at the site. The chamber would originally have been covered with a large mound of earth.

❡If you visit this site it is worth considering its great antiquity—around 5,000 years have passed since its construction, so it must rate as one of the oldest human artifacts in Herefordshire. This is an isolated and atmospheric place and it is not surprising to find legends associated with it. One such legend tells of Arthur killing a giant here.

POSITION: On the ridge which connects Merbach Hill and Dorstone Hill.
▷Ordnance Map (1:50000). Presteigne and Hay-on-Wye 148.
▷Ordnance Map (1:25000). Hay-on-Wye. Pathfinder 1016 (SO 24/34).
MAP REFERENCE: 318431.

ACCESS: A steep minor road surmounts Dorstone Hill to connect the villages of Dorstone (on the B4348 Hay-on-Wye to Peterchurch road) and Bredwardine (on the B4352 Hay-on-Wye to Clehonger road). Take this road out of either village and turn off near the top of the hill, along the lane signposted to Arthur's Stone.

# 21 Downton

## *A Marvel of the 'Picturesque'*

Richard Payne Knight (1750–1824) was a grandson of the great ironmaster Richard Knight (see Burrington). He built Downton Castle in the Gothic taste and used the nearby gorge as a dramatic backdrop for two fine bridges.

POSITION: Overlooking the Teme, five miles west of Ludlow.
▷ Ordnance Map (1:50000). Presteigne and Hay-on-Wye 148.
▷ Ordnance Map (1:25000). Ludlow. Pathfinder 951 (SO 47/57).
MAP REFERENCE: 448752 (parking place).

ACCESS: Take the A49 to Bromfield. Turn left along the A4113 towards Leintwardine and Knighton. About two miles on, turn left to Downton. After less than a mile you will go over a cross-roads and should park a few yards further on.
℄ Downton Castle and its grounds are not open to the public. However, the two-mile walk described below follows legitimate Public Rights of Way. Walk back to the crossroads and turn right, downhill until you reach Forge Bridge. The footpath you need to follow leads off to the right just before the bridge, and closely follows the Teme upstream. Follow the track uphill past a house to reach the edge of a wood, where you should double back along another (higher) track which passes directly below the terrace of Downton Castle. The track then descends gently towards Castle Bridge, from which point you will have to retrace your steps.

[33]

## 22 Eastnor

### Obelisk in Memory of a Lost Son

This tall monument, visible for many miles, was built in 1812 by the first Earl Somers in memory of his eldest son, who was killed in the Peninsular war at Burgos.

¶ The views from the promontory upon which the obelisk is built are superb. You can see the magnificent and extravagant mansion of Eastnor Castle (also dating from 1812) designed by Sir Robert Smirke, the architect of the British Museum. Also visible are the moat and ruins of Bronsil Castle, which dates from 1460.

¶ Eastnor Castle is regularly open to the public (check with the Tourist Office), but there is no public access to Bronsil Castle.

POSITION: Just north of the A438 Ledbury to Tewkesbury road, two and a half miles from Ledbury.

▷ Ordnance Map (1:50000). Worcester and The Malverns 150.

▷ Ordnance Map (1:25000). Ledbury and Much Marcle. Pathfinder 1041 (SO 63/73).

MAP REFERENCES: Obelisk: 752378; Eastnor Castle: 735368; Bronsil Castle: 749372.

ACCESS: Follow the A438 out of Ledbury towards Tewkesbury for about three miles to a point just beyond the brow of the Malvern Hills ridge, where you should turn left at a small and rather obscured crossroads. Follow this lane for about three quarters of a mile to the end of the wood on the left; at this point you should park and follow the footpath up through the wood and past the 'Gullet' quarry. At the crest of the hill you emerge into open countryside and continue in the same direction uphill to the obelisk.

# 23 Eastnor
## The Giant's Cave

Just below the crest of the Malvern Hills lies a small cave, about the size of a bus-shelter, hollowed out of the hard volcanic rock. The cave is referred to as the 'Giant's Cave' or 'Clutter's Cave'. Its age and origins are unknown, but there are many legends associated with it.

¶One story tells of a giant who lived in the cave and looked out one day to see his beautiful wife talking to another man on Colwall Green below. Jealously assuming this man to be a rival lover, the giant flung a huge stone at his wife, killing her instantly. Her remains are reputed to lie beneath the stone, Colwall Stone, which stands in the village of the same name.

¶The cave is a convenient shelter for the long-distance Malvern hillwalker in bad weather. It also provides an interesting objective at the end of a level walk with good views.

POSITION: On the Malvern Hills ridge between the A449 Ledbury to Great Malvern road and the A438 Ledbury to Tewkesbury road.
▷ Ordnance Map (1:50000). Worcester and The Malverns 150.
▷ Ordnance Map (1:25000). Ledbury and Much Marcle. Pathfinder 1041 (SO 63/73).
MAP REFERENCES: Cave: 762393; Colwall Stone: 755425.

ACCESS: The shortest and simplest approach to the cave is to start from the large car park opposite the hotel at the crest of the A449 Ledbury to Great Malvern road. Avoid both the steep path up to the British Camp and the road down to the reservoir and take instead the fairly level path which contours round the eastern flank of the Malvern Hills, below the British Camp. The cave is less than a mile along this path, at a point where you are following the crest of the ridge.

## 24 Eastnor
### *The Red Earl's Dyke*

The Shire Ditch or Red Earl's dyke is an embankment visible along parts of the Malvern Hills ridge. It is believed to have been built by Gilbert de Clare, the red-headed Earl of Gloucester, between 1287 and 1291. The Earl owned Malvern Chase and was in dispute with the Bishop of Hereford over the boundaries of their hunting forests. Having reached agreement that the boundary should follow the crest of the Malvern Hills, the Earl is said to have cunningly constructed the ditch and its associated fence to his own advantage. He did this by positioning the ditch and fence a few yards to the east of the ridge crest (i.e. on his side), which meant that the Bishop's deer could jump downhill onto the Earl's land without much difficulty, but there was little chance of any deer being able to jump uphill into the Bishop's hunting grounds.
❧ The ditch is well-preserved just south of Clutter's Cave.

POSITION: On the Malvern Hills ridge between the A449 Ledbury to Great Malvern road and the A438 Ledbury to Tewkesbury road.
▷ Ordnance Map (1:50000). Worcester and The Malverns 150.
▷ Ordnance Map (1:25000). Ledbury and Much Marcle. Pathfinder 1041 (SO 63/73).
MAP REFERENCE: 762390.

ACCESS: The shortest and simplest approach to the dyke is to start from the large car park opposite the hotel at the crest of the A449 Ledbury to Great Malvern road. Avoid both the steep path up to the British Camp and the road down to the reservoir and take instead the fairly level path which contours round the eastern flank of the Malvern Hills, below the British Camp. The dyke is noticeable after about a mile along this path, south of Clutter's Cave.

# 25 Eastnor

## The Curse of Raggedstone

Raggedstone Hill is part of the less well-known southern tail of the Malvern Hills ridge. Legend tells of a Monk from Little Malvern Priory (about three miles to the north) who fell in love with a local girl despite his vows of chastity. His punishment from the Prior was to crawl to the top of Raggedstone Hill every day on his hands and knees. Not surprisingly, the Monk tired of this and cursed the hill, and anyone on whom its shadow should fall. Victims have apparently included Cardinal Wolsey and Member of Parliament William Huskisson who was struck and killed by George Stephenson's 'Rocket' steam locomotive at its first public trial. It would therefore seem prudent to approach Raggedstone from the east in the morning and from the west in the afternoon!

POSITION: Raggedstone Hill rises immediately south of the A438 Ledbury to Tewkesbury road, about four miles from Ledbury.
▷ Ordnance Map (1:50000). Worcester and The Malverns 150.
▷ Ordnance Map (1:25000). Ledbury and Much Marcle. Pathfinder 1041 (SO 63/73).
MAP REFERENCE: 760364.

ACCESS: Parking space is available on the left hand side of the A449 Ledbury to Tewkesbury road, right opposite Raggedstone Hill. The Malvern Hills Conservators own only the eastern side of the hill, and a path ascends it from this side. The path starts from the main road at a point just over the brow and into Worcestershire.

INVICTÆ FIDELITATIS PREMIUM
THIS MEMORIAL COMMEMORATES
THOMAS WINTER

BORN AT RIDGE END FOWNHOPE HEREFORDSHIRE
FEBRUARY 22ND 1795 AND DIED AT THE
CASTLE TAVERN HOLBORN AUGUST 20TH 1851
BURIED AT WEST NORWOOD CEMETERY LONDON
ERECTED BY HIS COUNTRYMEN OF THE LAND
OF CIDER IN TOKEN OF THEIR ESTEEM FOR
THE MANLINESS AND SCIENCE WHICH IN
MANY SEVERE CONTESTS IN THE PUGILISTIC
RING UNDER THE NAME OF SPRING RAISED
HIM TO THE PROUD DISTINCTION OF THE
CHAMPION OF ENGLAND 1823–24
THOU MIGHTY MASTER OF THE MILLING SET
MORE POTENT FAR THAN MANY THAT HAVE MET
IN P.C. RING, MAY MARS, WHO WATCHES OER
THE HALF-STRIPPED VOTARIES OF THE SAWDUST FLOOR
PROTECT THEE STILL, AND ROUND THY LAURELS CLING
WHILE CRIBB, WITH IRON LUNGS, SHOUTS GO IT SPRING

# 26 Fownhope
## *Memorial to a Champion Boxer*

The memorial is in the form of a stone wheel and trough from a cider mill and commemorates Thomas Winter, a boxer better known as 'Tom Spring'. He was champion of England 1823-24. His popularity is indicated by the fact that the grandstand at Worcester racecourse collapsed under the weight of a large crowd during one of his fights in 1824. The memorial dates from the 1950s and is positioned in an idyllic spot amid the Woolhope hills, opposite the farm where he was born. The weathered inscription is reproduced on the facing page.

POSITION: In a field beside the Fownhope to Woolhope road.
▷ Ordnance Map (1:50000). Hereford and Leominster 149.
▷ Ordnance Map (1:25000). Hereford (South). Pathfinder 1040 (SO 43/53).
MAP REFERENCE: 588351.

ACCESS: Take the Woolhope road from central Fownhope (near the fire station). Just over a mile along this road you will see a signpost on the right pointing to 'Tom Spring Memorial' through a roadside gate, across a field and through another gate near a stream (about 100 metres).

# 27 Fownhope
## *Whipping Post and Stocks*

Imprisonment in the village stocks was a common punishment in the past. The stocks consist of a pair of hinged boards, each with arm/leg hollows cut out. The victim's limbs were placed in these cut-outs before the boards were closed together and locked. The stocks were often combined with a post, to which the unfortunate criminal could be secured for a whipping.

¶The stocks at Fownhope are well preserved; in 1909 they were placed in a protective shelter outside the churchyard wall. The last time they were used would have been long before this date; whipping became forbidden by law in 1791. Apparently, the Fownhope stocks were last used for a man named Winter, found guilty of drunkenness.

POSITION: Beside the B4224 at Fownhope.
▷Ordnance Map (1:50000). Hereford and Leominster 149.
▷Ordnance Map (1:25000). Hereford (South). Pathfinder 1040 (SO 43/53).
MAP REFERENCE: 582343.

ACCESS: Take the B4224 road from Hereford towards Ross. After about six miles you reach Fownhope church on the right hand side of the road. The stocks are just to the left of the gate to the churchyard, immediately next to the main road.

# 28 Foy
## A Parish Held Together by a Footbridge

Rivers and streams are often used as boundaries. Unusually, the parish of Foy is divided into two parts by a large loop of the River Wye, across which there is only one bridge. This is an attractive suspension footbridge built in 1876, and rebuilt in the 1930s. There is a considerable amount of (inbuilt) movement in the bridge as you walk across, but you should not be tempted to start large sways or ripples because this increases wear, and will incur the wrath of parishioners to whom the bridge is important—it does save a road journey of at least six miles.

POSITION: Alongside the minor road from Ross-on-Wye to How Caple, via Brampton Abbotts.
▷ Ordnance Map (1:50000). Hereford and Leominster 149.
▷ Ordnance Map (1:25000). Ross-on-Wye (East). Pathfinder 1065 (SO 62/72).
MAP REFERENCE: 604284.

ACCESS: Take the minor Brampton Abbotts road uphill from the 'Fiveways' junction at the lower end of Broad Street in Ross-on-Wye. The footbridge is right next to the road, about two and a half miles from Ross. You will see it as you descend a short but steep hill down towards the River Wye.

# 29 Garway
## An Ancient Dovecote and Unusual Church Remains

The dovecote dates from 1326 and is said to contain 666 nesting alcoves. The building is circular with a domed roof. It is linked historically with the nearby church of St Michael, which contains the excavated remains of a round nave. Garway was a preceptory of the Knight's Templars, and was founded in the late 1180s. The round nave was in memory of the Holy Sepulchre in Jerusalem.

POSITION: Just south of Garway church.
▷ Ordnance Map (1:50000). Abergavenny and the Black Mountains 161.
▷ Ordnance Map (1:25000). Ross-on-Wye (West). Pathfinder 1064 (SO 42/52).
MAP REFERENCE: 455224.

ACCESS: Take the A49/A466 Hereford to Monmouth road. About 11 miles from Hereford you should turn right along the B4521 towards Abergavenny. After a mile you come to the small settlement of Broad Oak, where you take the second right for Garway. Follow this lane across Garway Common, past 'The Moon' public house, until you reach a left turn in a dip—this is the location of the dovecote and church (about two miles from Broad Oak). The dovecote lies in a farmyard below the church. Footpaths cross the yard, but it would be diplomatic to ask for permission to enter the dovecote.

# 30 Hampton Bishop

## *An Isolated Bridge over the River Lugg*

Isolated amid the tranquility of the Lugg meadows stands an old stone bridge carrying a bridleway over the River Lugg. This bridleway must mark the course of an old route linking Longworth with Hampton Bishop. The modern road network avoids this area, which is subject to flooding.

⟪The Lugg meadows provide a refuge for wildlife and peace-seeking humans alike. Some parts are still managed using traditional methods. Unfortunately this area is under tremendous pressure from development, including gravel extraction and the planned A49 Hereford by-pass. The old Lugg bridge is a curiosity to visit sooner rather than later, before the atmosphere of its surroundings deteriorates.

POSITION: Half a mile north of the village of Hampton Bishop, which lies a mile south-east of the edge of Hereford, on the B4224 towards Ross-on-Wye.

▷ Ordnance Map (1:50000). Hereford and Leominster 149.

▷ Ordnance Map (1:25000). Hereford (South). Pathfinder 1040 (SO 43/53).

MAP REFERENCE: 558388.

ACCESS: There are three left turns from the B4224 into Hampton Bishop village. Take the second of these and park near the church. A public right of way leads from the left of the church, northwards to the old bridge, crossing a lane on the way.

# 31 Hereford
## *The Twisted Spire*

Most people have seen or heard of the twisted spire of the church in Chesterfield, Derbyshire, but Hereford has a lesser-known rival to this famous landmark!

❡The twist in the spire of All Saints is noticeable from many points in the city. The church was built in the late thirteenth or early fourteenth century on the line of an earlier ditch, which later led to subsidence. The twist to the spire developed at this point and the building had to be buttressed on its north side (Bewell Street).

POSITION: At the opposite end of Broad Street to the Cathedral.
▷ Ordnance Map (1:50000). Hereford and Leominster 149.
▷ Ordnance Map (1:25000). Hereford (North). Pathfinder 1017 (SO 44/54).
MAP REFERENCE: 509400.

ACCESS: Turn left coming out of the Tourist Office and head across pedestrianised High Town, and you will see the All Saints ahead of you.

# 32 Hereford
## St Ethelbert's Well

Ethelbert became King of the East Angles in 792. Strongly religious, he set out to marry Elfrida, a daughter of Offa, King of the Mercians. His rendezvous was at Offa's palace, now called Sutton Walls, a few miles north of Hereford. Jealous members of Offa's family organized Ethelbert's murder the night before his intended marriage. He thus became a martyr, who appeared as a vision and ordered the removal of his body to the site of Hereford Cathedral, where there was at that time a monastery.

⟨The story goes on to tell how a well gushed forth when the saint's body was laid to rest on the banks of the Wye. Hereford Civic Trust have restored a well near the Cathedral, and above it is a very weathered carved stone head, reputedly a representation of St Ethelbert wearing a crown. The water from the well was thought to be good for ulcers and sores. Any water you see coming out from today's well will be from the mains, to which it was connected during restoration.

POSITION: In the corner of Castle Green nearest the Cathedral.
▷ Ordnance Map (1:50000). Hereford and Leominster 149.
▷ Ordnance Map (1:25000). Hereford (South). Pathfinder 1040 (SO 43/53).
MAP REFERENCE: 511396.

ACCESS: The well is set into a high brick wall immediately to your left as you emerge into Castle Green from Quay Street. The latter is a narrow lane off the right hand side of Castle Street, soon after you leave the Cathedral precincts by the black painted iron gates at their eastern end.

## 33 Hoarwithy
### An Outstanding Italianate Church

St Catherine's church stands in a prominent position, and cannot fail to impress the visitor rounding the bend into the village of Hoarwithy. The building dates from the late nineteenth century and is built around an earlier church of 1843. The architect of the new church was J.P. Seddon, who chose a South Italian Romanesque and semi-Byzantine style. On a sunny day this gives Hoarwithy a Mediterranean feel. Both the inside and outside of the church have many delights for the connoisseur and amateur alike. My personal favourite is the approach to the entrance: up a long shady flight of steps from the road and through a most attractive cloister with a mosaic floor, a good place to sit and admire the view.
ℭBrockhampton-by-Ross (see separate entry) is only a few miles away. This part of the Wye valley is rich in evidence of the good work carried out by Victorian church architects.

POSITION: Hoarwithy lies by the River Wye, between Hereford and Ross-on-Wye.
▷Ordnance Map (1:50000). Hereford and Leominster 149.
▷Ordnance Map (1:25000). Ross-on-Wye (West). Pathfinder 1064 (SO 42/52).
MAP REFERENCE: 546294.

ACCESS: Initially take the A49 road towards Ross-on-Wye from Hereford, but turn left at the traffic lights by the 'Broad Leys' public house, along the B4399 towards Holme Lacy. After a short distance turn right along the minor road towards Hoarwithy, which you reach after about six miles.

# 34 Hope Mansell
## *The Dancing Green*

This delightful name originates from a maypole which used to be set up regularly at this attractive spot on the edge of the Forest of Dean, well off the beaten track. An added curiosity is that Dancing Green used to be in Gloucestershire, until a boundary change in the 1960s.

¶ An outdoor church service is still held every year on the green.

¶ There are many interesting short walks around this area of scattered houses and small enclosures, but you will need the 1:25000 O.S. map.

POSITION: Three miles south east of Ross-on-Wye.

▷ Ordnance Map (1:50000). Gloucester and Forest of Dean 162.

▷ Ordnance Map (1:25000). Ross-on-Wye East. Pathfinder 1065 (SO 62/72).

MAP REFERENCE: 635209.

ACCESS: Take the A40 road from Ross towards Gloucester. After about three miles you will reach the hamlet of Ryeford, at which point you should turn right to Pontshill. Take the second left turn (uphill) off this road, at a point where it bends to the right. Follow the winding lane uphill for just over half a mile and turn left at the crossroads. The Dancing Green is on the left of the road immediately after the first bend (in front of Red House Farm).

# 35 Hope Mansell
## *The Spoil Heap from a Gold Mine*

Remarkable though it may seem, in 1906 the 'Chastan Syndicate' was formed to exploit the small amounts of gold found in the Old Red Sandstone rock of this area. The exploratory Bailey Level was driven into the base of the steep western slope of Wigpool Common. Only six grains of gold per ton of rock were found, and the level was extended in search of iron ore in 1921. The mine entrance is still visible at the time of writing, but strictly speaking it lies in Gloucestershire, on the far side of the course of the Lea to Drybrook railway line. However, large amounts of spoil accumulated on the Herefordshire side of the border. I wish you good luck if you intend to sift through this!

POSITION: Near the settlement of Bailey Lane End.
▷ Ordnance Map (1:50000). Gloucester and Forest of Dean 162.
▷ Ordnance Map (1:25000). Cinderford and Forest of Dean (North). Pathfinder 1088 (SO 61/71).
MAP REFERENCE: 645196.

ACCESS: Take the A40 from Ross-on-Wye towards Gloucester. After about three miles, take the second turning on the right (towards Drybrook) after you have passed through Ryeford. This road leads to the scattered settlement at Bailey Lane End, through which you pass to enter a woodland area in which you soon encounter a left turn, which you should take. About 300 metres from the junction you will see the spoil heap on the right of the road amongst the trees. There is also a track ascending a short rise to the mine entrance.

# 36 Kentchurch
## The Bridge where the Devil was Tricked

'Jack o' Kent', who lived in the Kentchurch area, is a prominent figure in Herefordshire folk tales. We do not know who the original model for Jack was, but the three favourites are Owain Glyndwr, Sir John Oldcastle or Sion Cent, a Welsh poet.

⟨There is a legend regarding the original bridge over the Monnow at Kentchurch. Jack and the Devil built the bridge overnight, because that which they built by night fell down by day if it was not complete. The two workers had made a pact that the first person over the bridge would become the Devil's property. Jack saved a human soul from this fate by tempting a dog over after a shrewdly-tossed bone. The painted sign of the nearby public house reflects this legend.

⟨Watched over by the brooding bulk of Garway Hill, this area has an ancient, secret feel to it. It is not surprising that the legendary fugitives Owain Glyndwr and John Oldcastle are said to have hidden here. Both men were real people around whom legends grew up: Glyndwr was a rebellious Welsh freedom fighter who is believed to have 'retired' in 1415 to one or other of his daughters' homes (Monnington and Kentchurch) whilst Oldcastle (also known as Lord Cobham) was a much persecuted religious reformer, born in Herefordshire around 1360.

POSITION: On the River Monnow, beneath the western flank of Garway Hill.

▷Ordnance Map (1:50000). Abergavenny and The Black Mountains 161.

▷Ordnance Map (1:25000). Ross-on-Wye (West). Pathfinder 1064 (SO 42/52).

MAP REFERENCE: 411257.

ACCESS: Take the A465 road towards Abergavenny from Hereford as far as Pontrilas (about 12 miles) and turn left here along the B4347 towards Monmouth. Just over a mile along this road you come to a sharp right-hand bend by the gates to Kentchurch Court, just before crossing the Monnow bridge.

# 37 Kilpeck
## *Famous Norman Carvings*

The carved stone decorations on Kilpeck church are internationally famous. The carvings are exceptionally well preserved, after over eight hundred years of weathering. Humans, animals and monsters such as dragons abound. There is also a 'sheila-na-gig'—a female figure adopting a most uncompromising pose! The highlight is the south doorway, which includes a Tree of Life.

¶ Kilpeck displays the best preserved work of the 'Herefordshire School of Sculpture', which encompasses carvings found in churches at Shobdon, Rowlstone, Fownhope, Brinsop and Stretton Sugwas, and also some at Leominster. A possible explanation for this fine work in a remote corner of England is that Oliver de Merlimond, whilst building Shobdon church (c. 1140), went on a pilgrimage to the shrine of St James at Santiago de Compostela in Spain. Impressed by the architecture he saw *en route*, he may have brought back French craftsmen to work at Shobdon and elsewhere.

POSITION: Just south of the main A465 Hereford to Abergavenny road, about eight miles from Hereford.

▷ Ordnance Map (1:50000) Hereford and Leominster 149.

▷ Ordnance Map (1:25000) Hereford South. Pathfinder 1040 (SO 43/53).

ACCESS: Take the A465 from Hereford towards Abergavenny. After about eight miles turn left at a signpost to Kilpeck. After crossing the railway line, look out for a crossroads at which you should turn right. After 300 metres you reach the church, which has a small car park.

# 38 Kingsland
## Site of the Battle of Mortimer's Cross

The name of Mortimer's Cross will probably have stuck in many people's minds from history lessons at school. The battle, which took place on 2nd February 1461, led to the end of the Wars of the Roses and the establishment of the Yorkist line on the throne. The Yorkist force was led by Edward Mortimer, Earl of March and eldest son of the Duke of York. The Lancastrian force was led by Jasper Tudor, Earl of Pembroke. The slaughter was great on both sides, with four thousand dead. Edward emerged as the victor and was proclaimed King Edward IV on 5th March, at the age of nineteen.

❡The painted signs of the public house at Mortimer's Cross recall the battle, as does a monument erected in 1799, one mile south of the site. The battle has been restaged for the video camera by enthusiasts in period dress. The video and other information are available in Hereford Library. Otherwise, there is no trace of this bloody event in what is nowadays a quiet and empty corner of Herefordshire.

POSITION: Near the crossing of the A4110 and B4362, north-west of Leominster.
▷ Ordnance Map (1:50000). Hereford and Leominster 149.
▷ Ordnance Map (1:25000). Tenbury Wells and Mortimer's Cross. Pathfinder 972 (SO 46/56).
MAP REFERENCE: 426636 (monument 436619).

ACCESS: Take the A4110 road out of Hereford towards Knighton. You will reach Mortimer's Cross after about 17 miles. The site of the battle is the area lying between the A4110 and the River Lugg, south of the B4362.

# 39 Kington Rural
## The Legend of the Whet Stone

The Whet Stone is a large stone with a flat surface and rough sides lying on the summit of Hergest Ridge. It is believed that in the fourteenth century it was customary to place wheat and other cereals for sale around this stone. This may have been due to country people's reluctance to come right into town with their goods for sale, because of a fear of catching infectious diseases. It appears that the origin of the name 'Whet Stone' may be a shortened version of 'Wheat Stone'. Local wit must have led to the legend that the stone goes down to the water to 'whet' its thirst every morning, as the cock crows. Even if you fail to see the stone move, Hergest Ridge is a good place from which to watch the sun rise.

POSITION: High up on Hergest Ridge which is near Kington.
▷Ordnance Map (1:50000). Presteigne and Hay-on-Wye 148.
▷Ordnance Map (1:25000). Kington. Pathfinder 993 (SO 25/35).
MAP REFERENCE: 260568.

ACCESS: Take the A480 or A438/A4111 roads from Hereford to Kington. It is simplest to drive round the town's by-pass and turn left back towards the town at its western end. After a short rise you should turn right uphill towards Hergest Croft. This lane passes Hergest Croft and continues uphill, the road surface decreasing in quality. Eventually you will see a gate barring your way straight ahead. Park near here and continue on foot, through the gate and uphill along the grassy crest of the ridge to the Whet Stone (just over a mile from the gate).

# 40 Kington Rural
## *The Black Dog of Hergest*

Black Vaughan of Hergest Court and his dog are two of Hereford-shire's most famous ghosts. Black Vaughan is said to be the ghost of Thomas Vaughan, who has a monument in the Vaughan chapel of Kington church. History shows that he was a brave and honourable man, who was killed at the battle of Banbury in 1469. Legend has curiously presented him as a wicked man who could not rest after death, and so returned to terrify the local people in various forms, including a whirlwind and a black bull. There was no choice but to lay the spirit. This was achieved with the help of a stout-hearted parson, who managed to confine Vaughan's spirit in a snuff box, which was then buried in the bottom of Hergest pool.

❡ Black Vaughan's dog also returned to haunt the area as 'The Black Dog of Hergest'. The dog is said to haunt Hergest Ridge and a room at the top of Hergest Court. The appearance of the dog was said to herald a death in the Vaughan family.

❡ It is often said that the Black Dog of Hergest was the model for Sir Arthur Conan Doyle's *Hound of the Baskervilles*. Circumstantial evidence is provided by the existence of 'The Baskerville Arms' at Clyro, not far away, with the figure of a black dog above its porch. Regrettably, the evidence of Conan Doyle's biographers points to the fact that the famous story springs from a Dartmoor legend.

POSITION: Hergest Ridge is near Kington.
▷ Ordnance Map (1:50000). Presteigne and Hay-on-Wye 148.
▷ Ordnance Map (1:25000). Kington. Pathfinder 993 (SO 25/35).
MAP REFERENCE: Grid Square 2556.

ACCESS: Take the A480 or A438/A4111 roads from Hereford to Kington. It is simplest to drive round the town's by-pass and turn left back towards the town at its western end. After a short rise you should turn right uphill towards Hergest Croft. This lane passes Hergest Croft and continues uphill, the road surface decreasing in quality. Eventually you will see a gate barring your way straight ahead. Park near here and continue on foot, through the gate and uphill along the grassy ridge crest. It is possible to walk the length of the ridge to the village of Gladestry.

## 41 Ledbury Rural
### *The Big Viaduct over a Small River*

An impressive thirty-arched railway viaduct crosses the wide deep valley of the relatively small river Leadon. The viaduct carries the line from Hereford to Worcester, for which the contractors were Stephen Ballard (see Yarkhill) and Thomas Brassey. The viaduct was built in 1859-61. Over a million bricks were used in its construction.

⁋There is a sad story dating from the days of the 'blackout' during the Second World War. One dark night a train from Hereford to Worcester had stopped on the viaduct before entering Ledbury station; an unfortunate passenger assumed that the train was waiting at the platform and stepped out to his death.

⁋Another curiosity about Ledbury station is that it has the country's first privately-run booking office. For some years the station had been unmanned until a local businessman negotiated with British Rail to provide a service to the public.

POSITION: Just north-west of the town of Ledbury.
▷ Ordnance Map (1:50000). Hereford and Leominster 149.
▷ Ordnance Map (1:25000). Ledbury and Much Marcle. Pathfinder 1041 (SO 63/73).
MAP REFERENCE: 702387.

ACCESS: The viaduct may be viewed from the A438 Ledbury to Hereford road, soon after leaving the outskirts of the town; there is also a view from the new by-pass. Alternatively, you could make the crossing by train.

# 42 Ledbury
## Pride and Greed and some Relics of the Civil War

The airy, tranquil space of Ledbury's parish church contains evidence of the turbulent past of this area. The Civil War battle of Ledbury was fought in 1645, and the door on the west side of the Chapter House is riddled with holes which have been attributed to bullets. Beside the door is a glass case containing a sword reputed to have belonged to Major Backhouse, a Roundhead mortally wounded at the battle.

℄The church contains much else of interest, including carvings representing two of the seven deadly sins being overcome by the power of God. Pride is in the South Chapel and is represented by a winged dragon being attacked by the Lion of Judah. Greed is in the North Chapel and is shown by a manticore—a monster with a ravenous appetite for human flesh—which is being attacked by a winged lion. The carvings are thought to date from the first half of the fourteenth century.

POSITION: In St Michael and All Angels church, Ledbury.
▷ Ordnance Map (1:50000). Hereford and Leominster 149.
▷ Ordnance Map (1:25000). Ledbury and Much Marcle. Pathfinder 1041 (SO 63/73).
MAP REFERENCE: 713377.

ACCESS: It is best to park in one of Ledbury's car parks and walk to the church, since access by car is awkward and parking nearby is very restricted.

# 43 Leominster
## A Mobile Ducking Stool

Preserved in Leominster Priory church is a 'ducking stool'. This wheeled contraption consists of a long arm, pivoted in the middle, with a seat at one end. The ducking stool was a punishment reserved for 'scolding women' and for traders who gave short measure or adulterated food. The hapless victim was clamped into the chair and wheeled around the town before being submerged in a nearby stream or pond. It was much used at Leominster in the fifteenth and sixteenth centuries, and its last recorded use was in 1809.

POSITION: In Leominster Priory church.
▷ Ordnance Map (1:50000). Hereford and Leominster 149.
▷ Ordnance Map (1:25000). Leominster. Pathfinder 994 (SO 45/55).
MAP REFERENCE: 498593.

ACCESS: Park in one of Leominster's car parks and walk to the church (you should be able to pick out its tower).

# 44 Letton
## An 'Oxbow Lake'

An 'Oxbow Lake' is a feature formed by changes in a river's course across its floodplain. The narrow neck of a large loop of the river is breached, probably during a major flood. The main flow of water subsequently bypasses the loop, which is left as a stretch of still water marking the river's former course. In the case of the 'Horse Shoe Bend' at Letton, the parish boundary used to follow the former course of the River Wye through the lake (e.g. 1:50000 map, First Series, 1974). This means that a small uninhabited part of Bredwardine parish was cut off by the River Wye. Recently published maps show a realigned parish boundary which follows the present course of the river.

POSITION: In fields near Letton between the A438 Hereford to Brecon road and the River Wye.

▷ Ordnance Map (1:50000). Hereford and Leominster 149.

▷ Ordnance Map (1:25000). Hay-on-Wye. Pathfinder 1016 (SO 24/ 34).

MAP REFERENCE: Grid Squares 3345 and 3346.

ACCESS: There is no public access to the lake itself, but it can be clearly seen as one follows the A438 down into Letton coming from Hereford. An even better viewpoint is from the Knapp above Bredwardine (map reference 323446). This vantage point is accessible 500 metres along a public right of way leading off the steep lane behind Bredwardine at map reference 326444.

## 45 Little Birch
### A Glastonbury Thorn

The famous thorn at Glastonbury is said to have budded from the staff of Joseph of Arimathea, after his arrival there with the Holy Grail. There are many Holy thorn trees across Britain, said to have been grown from cuttings taken from the Glastonbury thorn. Herefordshire has its share of these trees, and the village of King's Thorn is named after one of them.

⟨The Holy thorns are said to blossom exactly at midnight on Twelfth Night (the time at which legend says that Christ was born). The tree I was shown by a local person was indeed starting to blossom when we visited it between Christmas and the New Year.

POSITION: In a garden at King's Thorn, about five miles south of Hereford.
▷ Ordnance Map (1:50000). Hereford and Leominster 149.
▷ Ordnance Map (1:25000). Hereford (South) and Area. Pathfinder 1040 (SO 43/53).
MAP REFERENCE: 509320.

ACCESS: Take the A49 road out of Hereford towards Ross. After about four miles, at the top of Callow Hill, turn left at the signpost to King's Thorn. After about three quarters of a mile, turn left again opposite a bus shelter. The King's Thorn area is an intricate maze of roads and tracks, and you will need careful navigation to find the tree. Ignore three right turns, and take the fourth, which branches off a long uphill straight. The lane you are now following has two sharp bends to the left, the second of which is a minor cross-roads, with an unsurfaced track leading straight ahead. You should park at this point—if there is a public house a little further along the surfaced road, you have found the right place!. Follow the unsurfaced road down to a turning area. The tree is over the garden boundary on the left, at a point where a narrow footpath leads off from the turning area.

# 46 Llangarron

## A Remarkable 'Misfit' Stream

If you have read the entry for Aymestry, you will know of the presence of ice in and around Herefordshire 20,000 years ago. As the climate began to warm up, the ice melted and released torrents of water which flowed away from the ice, carving valleys in the landscape as they did so. The large volumes of meltwater carved a deep, winding valley across South Herefordshire. This valley is now occupied by the Garren Brook, a small stream with small meanders following the course of the former torrent.

⟪From the vantage point located below, you will have a dramatic view across an amphitheatre-like sweep of a bend in the main valley, with the little stream wriggling around at the base. The evidence of the force of nature is impressive, as is the text-book clarity with which you can follow the sequence of geological events.

POSITION: Just outside the village of Llangarron.
▷ Ordnance Map (1:50000). Gloucester and Forest of Dean 162.
▷ Ordnance Map (1:25000). Ross-on-Wye (West). Pathfinder 1064 (SO 42/52).
MAP REFERENCE: 524208.

ACCESS: Take the A40 road towards Monmouth out of Ross-on-Wye and turn off right towards Glewstone about a mile beyond Wilton roundabout. Follow this road through Glewstone, across the A4137 and into Llangarron where you should turn left by the church and go uphill and stop just before the police house (about three miles from the Glewstone turn). The vista opens up on your left.

# 47 Longtown
## *The Sad Story of the 'Longtown Harriers'*

It has long been an insult to refer to an inhabitant of the Longtown area as a 'Clodock Courser' or a 'Longtown Harrier'. The reason goes back nearly a hundred years.

❡The incident happened on the freezing cold night of January 12th, 1893. During the day, there had been a funeral in the village after which a large crowd had repaired to the warmth of the Cornewall Arms in Clodock. Soon the cold and the funeral were forgotten and drinking and singing began. Most people had gone by nine o'clock, but a group of six men remained. Eventually, they staggered off to find William Prosser of Hunthouse Cottage, who had been at the inn earlier. They stood outside his cottage shouting and hammering at the door. Prosser tried to give them the slip but they caught him and rolled him in the snow. He broke away but was recaptured and thrown in the Monnow. By now Prosser was terrified. He ran for help at another cottage, but couldn't raise anyone. Convinced his pursuers were intent on killing him, he fled across the snow-covered fields. In the morning he was found hanging by his clothes on a cottage gate, frozen to death.

❡On March 3rd the six men were tried in Hereford for manslaughter. All pleaded guilty. Impressed by the evidence of their previous good character the judge imposed light sentences, the longest being one year in prison.

POSITION: Beside the River Monnow, just south of Longtown.
▷Ordnance Map (1:50000). Abergavenny and The Black Mountains 161.
▷Ordnance Map (1:25000). Longtown and Pandy. Pathfinder 1063 (SO 22/32).
MAP REFERENCE: 326275 (Cornewall Arms).

ACCESS: Take the A465 road from Hereford towards Abergavenny and turn right at Pandy (about eighteen miles from Hereford), under the railway line and on to Clodock (turn right to the village on a left-hand bend about three miles from Pandy). The incidents described above took place along the lane beyond the Cornewall Arms.

# 48 Lucton
## *A Landscape of 'Drumlins'*

This area, and much of the countryside to the south-west and north-east, is made up of a glacial deposit called 'Boulder Clay' which has been shaped by moving ice into low, elongated hillocks called 'Drumlins'. The distinctive landscape consists of a series of these drumlins with intervening hollows giving what is sometimes called 'basket of eggs' topography (imagine a basket of eggs with a cloth draped over the top). The general orientation of the drumlins, together with analysis of the orientation of stones within the boulder clay, clearly indicate ice movement in an easterly direction. The clearest impression of the drumlin landscape will be gained from a light aircraft, available at Shobdon airfield nearby.

POSITION: In fields to the left of the B4362 between Lucton and the River Lugg.
▷ Ordnance Map (1:50000). Hereford and Leominster 149.
▷ Ordnance Map (1:25000). Tenbury Wells and Mortimers Cross. Pathfinder 972 (SO 46/56).
MAP REFERENCE: Grid Square 4363.

ACCESS: A public right of way runs through the area from the bend in the lane at map reference 436641 to the road bridge over the Lugg at map reference 427637 (about one kilometre).

# 49 Lugwardine
## Memorial to a Horse

In the shade of a tree, overlooking Longworth Hall and the Frome valley, stand sad remains of an attractive stone urn. It may date back to before the eighteenth century, and is thought to be in memory of a horse. The urn was discovered in the 1880s in the cellar of Longworth Hall by the house's then owner, Henry Barneby. He restored it and placed it on a pillar in its present position.
¶The urn is now in pieces, presumably due to either vandalism, frost damage, or an accident with agricultural equipment. It is clear from the remains and from earlier photographs of the complete urn that this was an elegant piece of sculpture.

POSITION: In a field beside the lane from Bartestree to Longworth.
▷ Ordnance Map (1:50000). Hereford and Leominster 149.
▷ Ordnance Map (1:25000). Hereford (North). Pathfinder 1017 (SO 44/54).
MAP REFERENCE: 56404006 (8-figure for accuracy).

ACCESS: Take the A438 from Hereford towards Ledbury. After about four miles you will pass through the village of Bartestree and reach a crossroads at the crest of a long descent on the main road. You should turn right at this crossroads. The monument is visible through a gateway on the right after less than a mile, after you have passed the turning to Sheepcote farm. There is no public right of way to the monument, so you should either observe from a distance or seek permission from the landowner to have a closer look.

# 50 Mansell Lacy
## *The House with a Built-in Dovecote*

In the centre of Mansell Lacy village is an unusual house which incorporates a gable containing a large number of nesting alcoves with horizontal alighting ledges.

€Mansell Lacy is a village linked with the Foxley estate, which was the home of Sir Uvedale Price (1747–1829), a friend of Richard Payne Knight of Downton (see separate entry). Uvedale Price shared Knight's enthusiasm for the 'Picturesque' movement in landscaping, and although his house is no longer standing, much of the estate bears witness to his work. The estate is not open to the public.

POSITION: Just off the A480 Hereford to Kington road, about five miles from Hereford.
▷ Ordnance Map (1:50000). Hereford and Leominster 149.
▷ Ordnance Map (1:25000). Hereford (North). Pathfinder 1017 (SO 44/54).
MAP REFERENCE: 425456.

ACCESS: Take the A480 road out of Hereford towards Kington. After about five miles turn right along a lane signposted to Mansell Lacy (less than half a mile). The house with the dovecote is opposite the church, on the right of the drive to Foxley.

# 51 Mordiford
## The Spot where a Dragon was Slain

The Mordiford dragon is one of the best-known in English folk-lore. There are several versions of the story; one of them tells of a dragon which lived in woods near the village, killing the inhabitants and their cattle. The villagers offered a reward for the dragon's destruction, but this did not overcome anyone's fear until a condemned criminal, with nothing to lose, took the job on in exchange for a free pardon. The dragon was known to go down to the confluence of the Lugg and Wye to drink. The criminal hid at this place in an empty cider barrel. He succeeded in surprising and slaying the dragon, but was overcome himself by the dragon's last poisonous breath.

It seems that there was a painting of a dragon—possibly the wyvern (a two-legged dragon) from the coat of arms of the Priory of St Guthlac in Hereford, which once had the living of Mordiford in its gift, or possibly the wyvern which is the crest of the local Garston family—on the west wall of the church. This lasted from 1670 until restoration work in 1811 and may have stimulated local imagination to produce the legend. Whatever the case, traces of it can be seen to this day and the lane from Mordiford up into Haugh Wood is still known as 'Serpent's Lane'.

POSITION: Mordiford lies four and a half miles east of Hereford.
▷ Ordnance Map (1:50000). Hereford and Leominster 149.
▷ Ordnance Map (1:25000). Hereford (South). Pathfinder 1040 (SO 43/53).
MAP REFERENCE: 570374 (church); 565372 (Lugg/Wye confluence).

ACCESS: Take the B4224 road from Hereford towards Ross-on-Wye for about four and a half miles. The church is straight ahead as you cross Mordiford bridge.

# 52  Much Dewchurch
## *Tram Inn*

This oddly-named public house acquired its name from the horse-drawn tramroad, next to whose track it stands. A tramroad consisted of parallel L-section plates, along which 'trams' (trucks) with plain wheels were guided (by contrast, railways have plain rails guiding L-section wheels).

¶The tramway was originally constructed between 1811 and 1829 to carry coal from Govilon wharf (near Abergavenny) to Hereford.

¶The Tram Inn was once owned by the Hereford Railway Company. One of the easiest places to see the tramway itself is near its original terminus in Hereford.

### *Tram Inn*

POSITION: Beside the B4348, at a point where the railway line intersects at a level crossing, five miles south-west of Hereford.

▷ Ordnance Map (1:50000). Hereford and Leominster 149.

▷ Ordnance Map (1:25000). Hereford (South). Pathfinder 1040 (SO 43/53).

MAP REFERENCE: 464335.

ACCESS: Take the A465 out of Hereford towards Abergavenny and turn left after five miles, at Lock's Garage (B4348—signposted to Ross-on-Wye). The Tram Inn is half a mile down this road.

### *Tramroad*

POSITION: To the left of the footpath which follows the south bank of the Wye, upstream from the old bridge.

▷ Ordnance Map (1:50000). Hereford and Leominster 149.

▷ Ordnance Map (1:25000). Hereford (South). Pathfinder 1040 (SO 43/53).

MAP REFERENCE: 505394.

ACCESS: Start opposite the Saracen's Head pub and walk along the footpath on the south side of the Wye, towards the new concrete road bridge. On your left is the site of the terminus of the tramroad. Once you have passed under the new bridge, you should be able to see the low embankment of the tramroad which curves gradually away on your left, to pass behind the nearby school buildings.

## 53 Much Dewchurch
### Visits from a Ghost Story Writer

Montague Rhodes James is well known as the author of some of the best ghost stories ever written. *Ghost Stories of an Antiquary* was published by Edward Arnold in 1904 and includes 'The Mezzotint', 'Oh Whistle and I'll Come to You, My Lad', and 'Lost Hearts', all of which have been adapted for television in recent years.

He frequently visited Gwen McBryde, the widow of a friend, at Woodlands, in Herefordshire. During one of his visits he was invited to read the lesson at Abbey Dore, one of his favourite churches. In 1916 a visit to Herefordshire inspired him to write a story for Gwen's daughter Jane called 'The Five Jars'.

In the preface to *The Ghost Stories of M.R. James*, published in 1931, the author tells us that Herefordshire was the imagined scene of 'A View from a Hill', whilst 'The Stalls of Barchester Cathedral' is partly based on Hereford Cathedral.

POSITION: 'Woodlands' lies in the grounds of a now deserted mansion called 'The Mynde', near Much Dewchurch. It is a private house, but public rights of way lead across the park and up through Mynde Wood to Orcop Hill.

▷ Ordnance Map (1:50000). Hereford and Leominster 149.

▷ Ordnance Map (1:25000). Ross-on-Wye (West). Pathfinder 1064 (SO 42/52).

MAP REFERENCE: 470294.

ACCESS: Take the A465 road from Hereford towards Abergavenny. Turn left onto the B4348 at Lock's Garage, after about four and a half miles. Continue for a further two and a half miles into the village of Much Dewchurch, where you should park. It is possible to complete a circular walk via Bryngwyn, The Mynde and Woodlands, but you are well-advised to take the Pathfinder map with you.

# 54 Much Marcle
## 'The Wonder'

'The Wonder' is an area of disturbed ground on the side of Marcle Hill, marking the point where a major landslide occurred in 1575. It began during the evening of 17th February.

> Near the conflux of the Lugg and the Wye, eastward, a hill they call Marcley Hill in the year 1575 roused itself, as it were, out of sleep, and for three days together, shoving its prodigious body forwards with a horrible roaring noise and overturning all that stood in its way, advanced itself, to the astonishment of all beholders, to a higher station, by that kind of earthquake the which the naturalists call Brasmatia.

The landslip is said to have destroyed the chapel at Kynaston, together with hedges, trees and many cattle, affecting a total of twenty six acres.

◖The layers of rock which make up this east-facing slope dip steeply in the same direction. During February, one would expect the ground to be waterlogged and liable to slip.

POSITION: On the east-facing flank of Marcle Hill.
▷ Ordnance Map (1:50000). Hereford and Leominster 149.
▷ Ordnance Map (1:25000). Ledbury and Much Marcle. Pathfinder 1041 (SO 63/73).
MAP REFERENCE: 633365.

ACCESS: Take the B4224 road from Hereford towards Ross-on-Wye. After four miles you cross the River Lugg and enter the village of Mordiford, where you should take the second left turn, on the corner by 'The Moon' public house. Follow this lane up through Haugh Wood and down into Woolhope village (about three miles). At the 'T' junction turn left and follow the priority road down past the 'Butcher's Arms' public house, through a small housing estate, past a telephone kiosk and uphill to a fenced-in reservoir on your right (about a mile and a half). Turn right at the next junction, towards Much Marcle. About six hundred metres down this lane you will reach a left turn, and the remains of the landslip are through a gap in the bank on the right.

# 55 Much Marcle

## The Tree You Can Sit Inside

Outside the porch of Much Marcle church stands a beautiful old yew tree. Its girth is thirty-three feet, which has led to an estimate of it being four hundred years old. At some stage the centre of the tree must have rotted and been removed, so the trunk now consists of an arc of smaller stems encircling a hollow centre in which a seat has been placed. An arrangement of cast iron pillars supporting a circular rail holds up the spreading lower branches of the tree.
❦The church itself is full of interest, particularly the tombs, which include an unusual wooden effigy carved from a solid block of oak. A good, detailed guide book is available in the church.

POSITION: Much Marcle lies just off the main road from Ross-on-Wye to Ledbury.
▷ Ordnance Map (1:50000). Hereford and Leominster 149.
▷ Ordnance Map (1:25000). Ledbury and Much Marcle. Pathfinder 1041 (SO 63/73).
MAP REFERENCE: 657327

ACCESS: Take the A449 road out of Ross-on-Wye towards Ledbury. Turn sharp right along the B4024 at Weston's Garage (about seven miles from Ross-on-Wye) and the lane to the church leads off on the right after about five hundred metres.

# 56 Pembridge
## A Wooden Bell-House

Pembridge has the finest of Herefordshire's seven detached belfries. The style is similar to that found in Scandinavia and is very unusual for this part of the country, being more familiar in eastern counties such as Essex.

⟨The belfry dates from the fourteenth century. It has been suggested that it was built to support the bells whilst the church was under construction, and that a tower was never built on the church, perhaps because of a lack of money.

⟨Five bells are supported in a sturdy timber frame thought to date from the seventeenth century.

⟨It seems that the belfry may have served as a place of refuge in the past. There are narrow windows in the thick stone walls at its base, and the holes in the wooden door are said to have been made by shot. Once inside there is certainly a sense of security, and the scale and strength of the timber structure is most impressive.

POSITION: Adjacent to Pembridge church.
▷Ordnance Map (1:50000). Hereford and Leominster 149.
▷Ordnance Map (1:25000). Kington. Pathfinder 993 (SO 25/35).
MAP REFERENCE: 390580

ACCESS: Take the A44 road from Leominster towards Kington. Pembridge is about seven miles along this road, and the church is on the left in the village centre. The belfry is usually open during reasonable hours.

# 57 Peterchurch
## The Fish with the Gold Chain

The church of St Peter contains a strange sculpture of a fish with a
gold chain around its head. The sculpture is said to commemorate
the catch of such a fish in a nearby well called Golden Well.

POSITION: In St Peter's church, Peterchurch. The village lies about
12 miles west of Hereford.
▷ Ordnance Map (1:50000). Hereford and Leominster 149.
▷ Ordnance Map (1:25000). Pathfinder 1039 (SO 23/33).
MAP REFERENCE: 345385.

ACCESS: Take the A465 road out of Hereford towards Abergavenny, but turn right just after Belmont Abbey, along the B4352
towards Hay-on-Wye. Turn left in Clehonger (signposted Peterchurch) and at Kingstone you reach the B4348, which you turn right
onto. Turn left to the church in the centre of Peterchurch village.
The fish is inside the church, fixed high up on the wall opposite
the door.

# 58 Pipe and Lyde
## The Centre of Herefordshire

Right next to the main road stands a small stone monument and some trees planted to mark the geographical centre of Herefordshire. The inscription reads:

THESE TREES WERE
PLANTED BY
WILLIAM JAY
AND A FEW FRIENDS
TO MARK THE
CENTRE
OF THE COUNTY
APRIL 1857

While today's heavy traffic makes this a rather unpleasant spot to spend any time, you may wish to pay one visit and from that point on remember your central position whenever you pass this spot.

POSITION: On the right hand verge of the A49 Hereford to Leominster road.
▷ Ordnance Map (1:50000). Hereford and Leominster 149.
▷ Ordnance Map (1:25000). Hereford (North). Pathfinder 1017 (SO 44/54).
MAP REFERENCE: 504436.

ACCESS: Take the A49 road out of Hereford towards Leominster. About one and a quarter miles beyond the 'Starting Gate' roundabout you reach the crest of a long gentle incline, and the stone is on the right, just beyond the drive to a house. This is a dangerous place to park your car and walk around, so it is best to drive a little further, find a safe parking place and walk back up the roadside verge.

## 59 Ross-on-Wye
### The Old Prison

The origins of this square building cannot be mistaken; it was the town prison from 1838 to 1844, and its barred lancet windows and heavy studded door give it a suitably grim air. It stands to the right of Pig Alley, an ancient footway which winds up to High Street through one of the oldest parts of Ross—well worth exploring!

POSITION: On the south side of New Street, Ross-on-Wye.
▷ Ordnance Map (1:50000). Gloucester and Forest of Dean 162.
▷ Ordnance Map (1:25000). Ross-on-Wye (West). Pathfinder 1064 (SO 42/52).
MAP REFERENCE: 599243.

ACCESS: Park in one of the town car parks. New Street is the first left turning off Broad Street as you walk downhill from the Market House.

# 60 Ross-on-Wye
## *The Gazebo Tower*

This interesting round tower is incorporated into the medievalised northern edge of the Prospect. During the 1830s much work was carried out in this part of the town, and it remains a distinctive feature in the familiar view of the town from the bridge on the main Birmingham to South Wales road.

⟨ Wilton Road was cut into the steep red cliffs and is overlooked by the Gazebo Tower, which in turn stands in front of the Royal Hotel; all of them date from the same period.

POSITION: On the north-western edge of the town of Ross, overlooking the River Wye.

▷ Ordnance Map (1:50000). Gloucester and Forest of Dean 162.
▷ Ordnance Map (1:25000). Ross-on-Wye (West). Pathfinder 1064 (SO 42/52).

MAP REFERENCE: 597242.

ACCESS: Approaching Ross from Wilton roundabout, you will cross the River Wye on Wilton Bridge and approach the red cliffs, at which point the road bends to the left. Shortly after negotiating this bend you should turn off to the right, uphill towards the Royal Hotel; you may be able to park on the left shortly after turning off the main road.

# 61 Ross-on-Wye
## *The Banjo Player's Grave*

Harry Diamond was a widely known popular singer, who accompanied himself on his banjo. He lived at the turn of the century, and made Ross his home during the winter months, when he wasn't performing in resorts elsewhere. He was by all accounts a genial and kind-hearted man, as well as a very accomplished musician. He died in 1907 at the early age of thirty-three, a victim of heart disease and dropsy. His gravestone features a banjo with a broken string.

POSITION: In St Mary's churchyard, Ross-on-Wye.
▷ Ordnance Map (1:50000). Gloucester and Forest of Dean 162.
▷ Ordnance Map (1:25000). Ross-on-Wye (West). Pathfinder 1064 (SO 42/52).
MAP REFERENCE: 598241.

ACCESS: Park in one of the town car parks and walk to St Mary's church by following High Street westwards from the Market House, and then turning left up narrow Church Street. The simplest way to find the grave is to walk into the walled Prospect garden and exit via the pedimented gate (1700) to the south. After descending a short flight of steps you should walk straight ahead through the graves until you meet another path at a 'T' junction beneath a large chestnut tree; the back of Harry Diamond's prominent white gravestone should now be visible to your right.

# 62 Saint Margarets

## *A Beautiful Carved Wooden Rood Screen*

The little church of Saint Margarets is tucked away amongst a maze of little-used lanes in the foothills of the Black Mountains. The exterior of the building is unassuming, but inside is a breathtakingly beautiful carved wooden rood screen.

¶The screen dates from about 1520, and is in the form of a loft whose coving rests on two posts. The quality of the woodcarving is outstanding, with much running ornament, including vine and oak foliage. The posts have niches cut into them, in which figures of the Blessed Virgin and St John would have stood. At one time, the screen would have been brightly painted and gilded. The screen is of a Welsh type, of which only a few examples remain in the borders, the nearest being Partrishow in the Black Mountains.

¶Its existence is particularly fortunate since in 1547, after the Reformation, an order was made to destroy all images, and a great many churches lost their roods at this time.

N.B. At the time of writing, the public house next to the church is closed (you may notice it on the O.S. maps).

POSITION: Between Vowchurch and Longtown, on the ridge of high ground separating the Escley Brook and the River Dore.
▷ Ordnance Map (1:50000). Hereford and Leominster 149.
▷ Ordnance Map (1:25000). Golden Valley. Pathfinder 1039 (SO 23/33).
MAP REFERENCE: 353337.

ACCESS: The simplest approach is to take the A465 road to Abergavenny out of Hereford. Two miles out you should turn right onto the B4349/B4348 towards Peterchurch. This later involves a left turn in Clehonger, and a right turn at a 'T' junction beyond Kingstone. Soon after you have passed a left turn to Ross (the B4347) the road descends into a hollow where there is a rather obscured cross-roads, at which you should turn left towards Michaelchurch Escley. After passing through Vowchurch and Turnastone the road climbs steadily. About two miles beyond Turnastone, look out for the first left turn to St Margarets. The church is about two miles down this lane, on the inside of a sharp right-hand bend.

# 63 Sellack

## Obscure Suspension Footbridge over the River Wye

The only direct link between the parishes of Sellack and King's Caple is an elegant suspension bridge which enables pedestrians to cross the Wye. The bridge has a beautiful secluded setting amidst wide water meadows, and it is well worth seeking out. The best approach is from King's Caple, which enables you to take a short, pleasant walk across the meadows to Sellack church (see following entry). It is said that before this bridge was built, the Vicar used stilts to cross the river.

POSITION: South of the village of King's Caple, between Hereford and Ross.

▷Ordnance Map (1:50000). Hereford and Leominster 149.

▷Ordnance Map (1:25000). Ross-on-Wye West. Pathfinder 1064 (SO 42/52).

MAP REFERENCE: 565280 (the bridge falls on the join between 1:50000 O.S. map sheets 149 and 162).

ACCESS: Take the A49 road towards Hereford from Ross. Shortly after Wilton roundabout take a right turn signposted to Hoarwithy. Follow the road through to Hoarwithy village and then turn right just below the church and immediately fork right again to cross Hoarwithy bridge. Pass a right and a left turn before turning right to King's Caple. Go straight across at the crossroads and downhill to a sharp left hand bend where you should park (taking care not to obstruct any gateways). The footpath leading off from this point is overhung with trees, so you will not immediately realise that you are within a few yards of the suspension bridge. Once on the bridge, the way across the meadows to Sellack church is obvious.

# 64 Sellack

## A Very Simple Epitaph

Sellack church must be one of the most secluded in the country. In its peaceful churchyard you will find a stone cross with an embossed hand pointing upwards; underneath is the word 'GONE'. What more needs to be said?

POSITION: In Sellack churchyard, close to the eastern end of the church.
▷ Ordnance Map (1:50000). Gloucester and Forest of Dean 162.
▷ Ordnance Map (1:25000). Ross-on-Wye (West). Pathfinder 1064 (SO 42/52).
MAP REFERENCE: 565276.

ACCESS: Take the A49 road from Ross-on-Wye towards Hereford and take the second right turn after Wilton roundabout (less than half a mile, signposted Hoarwithy). Follow the priority road for two miles to Pict's Cross, where you should turn right and then look for a left turn down to Sellack church after about three quarters of a mile. A very pleasant alternative is to walk across the footbridge from King's Caple (see previous entry); you will see Sellack church ahead, across the meadows.

# 65 Shobdon

## The Unidentified Architect and the Curious Fate of the Norman Carvings

In the mid-eighteenth century, this Norman church was restored by an unidentified architect in a 'Strawberry Hill Gothic' style. ⟨Much of the original twelfth century carving was removed from the church and set up as 'Shobdon Arches'. Later, pinnacles, battlements and gables were added to this eye-catcher.

POSITION: Shobdon lies approximately seven miles north-west of Leominster.
▷ Ordnance Map (1:50000). Hereford and Leominster 149.
▷ Ordnance Map (1:25000). Tenbury Wells and Mortimer's Cross. Pathfinder 972 (SO 46/56).
MAP REFERENCES: 401628 (Shobdon church); 401632 (Shobdon Arches).

ACCESS: Take the A4110 from Hereford towards Knighton and turn left at Mortimer's Cross (see separate entry) along the B4362 towards Presteigne. Take the second right turn, after half a mile, and after a further half a mile go straight across the crossroads and up the drive to Shobdon church. If you miss the first turning off the B4362, keep on until the village of Shobdon, where a right turn leads up to the church.

# 66 Turnastone
## *An Unusual Enamel Sign*

Enamel advertisements have become collectors' items, so much so that reproductions are now produced. At Turnastone a notable original sign has been preserved on the wall of a house which also serves as a filling station. The large green, white and black sign advertises the Raleigh 'All Steel' bicycle, and is something of a local landmark. The filling station itself is unusual, in that the old-style petrol pumps are located behind the garden wall.

¶ Turnastone is an unusual name, as is Vowchurch, which lies on the opposite bank of the River Dore. A popular explanation is that the twin churches were built by two rival sisters, one of whom said to the other: 'I *vow* I will build my *church* before you can *turnastone* of yours'. The more likely explanation is that 'vow' means multi-coloured, and 'Turnastone' may be derived from an old English word for a thorn thicket.

POSITION: Turnastone lies about ten miles west of Hereford.
▷ Ordnance Map (1:50000). Hereford and Leominster 149.
▷ Ordnance Map (1:25000). Golden Valley. Pathfinder 1039 (SO 23/33).
MAP REFERENCE: 357364.

ACCESS: Take the A465 road towards Abergavenny out of Hereford. Turn right after two miles, onto the B4349/B4348 towards Peterchurch. This involves a left turn in Clehonger, and a right turn at a 'T' junction beyond Kingstone. Soon after you have passed a left turn to Ross-on-Wye (the B4347) the road descends into a hollow where there is a rather obscured cross-roads, at which you should turn left towards Michaelchurch Escley. In less than half a mile you will pass the filling station at Turnastone, on the left as you approach a sharp right hand bend.

# 67 Walford
## The Valley Without a River

The wooded hills of Chase and Penyard form an attractive back-drop to the town of Ross-on-Wye. The hills rise to over six hundred feet and are geologically part of the Forest of Dean. However, the hills are cut off from the rest of Dean by a wide, deep valley which runs from Weston-under-Penyard to Walford. This valley contains a tiny stream, which could not have cut such a large swathe through the countryside.

¶The explanation of this anomaly is that the River Wye once flowed in a huge loop around the site of Chase and Penyard. The course of this loop can be traced with the aid of the O.S. 1:50000 map. Starting from the horseshoe bend at Ross-on-Wye, the river would have crossed the site of Ross-on-Wye and flowed eastwards past the site of Weston-under-Penyard. It would then have swung in a right hand bend across the sites of Ryeford, Frogmore, Parkfields, Cobrey Park and Coughton. At this point it would have swung north and over the sites of Tudorville and Ashfield back to the horseshoe bend at Ross. Eventually, the neck of this huge loop was breached at Ross (also see entry for Letton) and the Wye assumed its present course, leaving its former valley virtually dry.

POSITION: The valley lies beyond Chase and Penyard hills, about two miles south of Ross-on-Wye.
▷Ordnance Map (1:50000). Gloucester and Forest of Dean 162.
▷Ordnance Map (1:25000). Ross-on-Wye (East). Pathfinder 1065 (SO 62/72).
MAP REFERENCES: Grid Squares 6021, 6121 and 6221.

ACCESS: You will follow the former course of the River Wye if you take the following route. Take the A40 road out of Ross-on-Wye towards Gloucester. After three miles, turn right to Pontshill. Follow the priority road which leads through the valley described above to Coughton, where you should turn right along the B4228 back into Ross.

## 68 Walford

### *Relic of a Forgotten Brew*

Beside the door of the 'New Buildings' pub is an enamel sign advertising 'Golden Hop' Pale Ale, brewed by the Alton Court Brewery Company in Station Street, Ross-on-Wye.

℄The brewery was established in 1846 and closed in 1956, after a takeover by the Stroud Brewery. 'Golden Hop' was one of two beers, '. . . brewed especially for Private Families', and sold at one and tuppence a gallon (much less than one new penny per pint!).

POSITION: The 'New Buildings' is an isolated pub at Forest Green, three miles south of Ross-on-Wye.

▷Ordnance Map (1:50000). Gloucester and Forest of Dean 162.

▷Ordnance Map (1:25000). Cinderford and Forest of Dean (North). Pathfinder 1088 (SO 61/71).

MAP REFERENCE: 601196.

ACCESS: Take the B4228 out of Ross. After a mile and a half, turn left where the main road bends right. Turn right to Howle Hill and right at the first cross-roads. Fork left at the next junction; the 'New Buildings' appears almost immediately on your left.

# 69 Walterstone
## The Abandoned Garden

On top of the ridge above Walterstone, overlooking the Black Mountains, lies an earthwork known as 'The Camp'. The curiosity of this place lies inside the ramparts, where you will find a very wild and overgrown garden covering several acres. On my visit, several planted trees and shrubs were identifiable including False Acacia, Bamboo, Tulip Tree, Azalea, Magnolia, and Copper Beech.

⟨This is a wonderful place to visit when the plants are in flower and the sun is out. The origin of the garden is perhaps best left a mystery, as this adds to the atmosphere of the place.

POSITION: In the remote south-west corner of Herefordshire, about sixteen miles from Hereford.

▷Ordnance Map (1:50000). Abergavenny and The Black Mountains 161.

▷Ordnance Map (1:25000). Longtown and Pandy. Pathfinder 1063 (SO 22/32).

ACCESS: Take the A465 road from Hereford towards Abergavenny and turn right at Pandy (about eighteen miles from Hereford). Go underneath the railway bridge and after a quarter of a mile, turn right at a cross-roads towards Walterstone. After crossing the River Monnow, ignore the road to Walterstone village and turn right. After just over a mile, a strip of common land opens out on your left, and you should park here. You will see a gate to the right of the first house on the common. Go over this gate and follow the public right of way about two hundred yards up to the edge of the camp, at which point you will see a track leading off to the left through a belt of woodland into the 'garden'.

# 70 Welsh Bicknor
## *Monument to a Family Tragedy*

In an isolated beauty spot stands a monument to a sixteen year-old boy drowned in the Wye nearby. Surrounded by rusty railings and overgrown by brambles, the inscription, framed by sculpted stalactites, tells the sad story:

SACRED TO THE MEMORY OF JOHN WHITEHEAD WARRE
Who perished near this Spot whilst bathing in the River Wye in sight of his
Parents Brother and Sisters on the 14th of September 1804
In the 16th year of his Age
GOD'S WILL BE DONE

There follows a long and moving inscription.

POSITION: On a remote stretch of river bank, two miles due south of Goodrich village.
▷ Ordnance Map (1:50000). Gloucester and Forest of Dean 162.
▷ Ordnance Map (1:25000). Monmouth. Pathfinder 1087 (SO 41/51).
MAP REFERENCE: 571161.

ACCESS: Goodrich village is five miles from Ross-on-Wye via the A40 (exit left after Pencraig) or the B4228/B4229 (turn right over Kerne Bridge). Descend the hill from the village along the B4229 towards Whitchurch. After half-a-mile turn left towards Symonds Yat (East) and Coleford. You will very soon reach Huntsham Bridge, where you should park unobtrusively. From the Goodrich side of the bridge, follow the riverside footpath upstream, with Coppet Hill on your left (i.e. walk southwards along the river's eastern bank). After about two miles you will enter a wood, and you will need to keep watch on the left-hand side of the path, or you will miss the monument; it lies slightly above the path, but only a few yards from it. If you leave the wood without finding the monument, you should retrace your steps.

# 71 Welsh Newton
## *The Saint's Grave*

In 1678 a certain Titus Oates claimed to have discovered a 'Popish Plot' to kill King Charles II. Details about the plot were vague, but a wild panic ensued as accusations were made against various Catholics. 30,000 of them fled from London, and the excitement did not by-pass Hereford. John Kemble was the resident Catholic priest to the Scudamore family at Pembridge Castle. Although over eighty, he was arrested and tried for complicity in the plot, before being hanged on Widemarsh Common on August 22, 1679. He was buried in Welsh Newton churchyard, where his gravestone remains. Oates was later exposed as a liar, and John Kemble was canonised on October 25, 1970.

POSITION: Beside the A466 Hereford to Monmouth road, at Welsh Newton.
▷ Ordnance Map (1:50000). Gloucester and Forest of Dean 162.
▷ Ordnance Map (1:25000). Monmouth. Pathfinder 1087 (SO 41/51).
MAP REFERENCE: 499180.

ACCESS: Take the A49 Ross road out of Hereford. Soon after the top of Callow Hill you should turn right onto the A466 towards Monmouth. You reach Welsh Newton two and a half miles after crossing the B4521 Abergavenny to Ross road. The church is on the left of the road, and access is via the lane which turns off on this side. John Kemble's grave is in the higher part of the churchyard, east of the church, near the preaching cross. The distinctive slab has a large crack across it, and is surrounded by a modern stone edge.

## 72 Whitbourne
### A Vinegar Baron's Mansion

Edward Bickerton Evans (1819–93) worked in the family business, the Hill Evans Vinegar works in Worcester (founded 1830). The company diversified into British wine, and by 1903 their factory was the biggest in the world. Edward was a great traveller and his house, Whitbourne Hall, was built in a Greek style, based on the Erechtheum. He was clearly a wealthy man: the tender for the house (built 1861–2) was £21,055. In 1876, Edward was listed in *The Great Landowners of Great Britain and Ireland* with 2,586 acres at a gross annual value of £4,000.

❡ The architect for Whitbourne Hall was E.W. Elmslie (1819–89), who also designed several buildings in Malvern. The house has many interesting features, both inside and out. Clearly visible on the west front are the remains of a gigantic bowed conservatory, which once had a rounded iron and glass roof. This part of the house may have been designed by another architect, R.L. Roumieu (1814–77). The high cost of heating the conservatory led to its abandonment.

❡ The house is not open to visitors, but is surrounded by drives and public footpaths, along which you may have a very pleasant walk.

POSITION: North of the A44 Leominster to Worcester road, in the far east of the county.
▷ Ordnance Map (1:50000) Hereford and Leominster 149.
▷ Ordnance Map (1:25000) Bromyard, Pathfinder 995 (SO 65/75).
MAP REFERENCE: 704568.

ACCESS: Take the A44 from Bromyard towards Worcester. After crossing Bringsty Common, you descend the hill towards Whitbourne. Four and a half miles from Bromyard you should turn left by a pub and drive for a mile, bearing left at two junctions, until you reach the northern lodge gates (near which you should park) and the drive to Whitbourne Hall. The Ordnance Survey map will be useful in locating this place and the walks around it.

# 73 Whitchurch
## An Unusual Way to Cross the River

Whitchurch can lay claim to the two most unusual crossings on the River Wye. There is the ferry at Symond's Yat; and there is a less well-known crossing at Biblins, a little further downstream. The Biblins crossing is in the form of a rope bridge slung between two wooden towers. The ropes are in fact strong steel hawsers, and a degree of rigidity has been given to the structure by lining its base and sides with a close steel mesh. There is a great deal of inbuilt movement when the bridge is in use, and the view of the river directly beneath your feet makes the crossing an exciting experience.

℄ Biblins itself is a very attractive spot, although it can be busy on a sunny day in summer. If this puts you off, the drama of the crossing is enhanced by a winter flood, so save your visit until then.

POSITION: About nine miles south-west of Ross-on-Wye.

▷ Ordnance Map (1:50000). Gloucester and The Forest of Dean 162.

▷ Ordnance Map (1:25000). Monmouth. Pathfinder 1087 (SO 41/51).

MAP REFERENCE: 549144.

ACCESS: Take the A40 dual carriageway towards Monmouth from Ross-on-Wye. After about six miles look out for the left turn to Whitchurch and Symonds Yat beside a fire station. Having taken this turning, you immediately encounter a roundabout, where you should turn right (second exit). Before the next flyover turn left to Crocker's Ash and the Doward. Drive parallel to the dual carriageway until you reach a left turn on to the Doward, next to the Doward Hotel. You are now on a very minor road which winds uphill for half a mile to a 'T' junction, where you should turn right. After another half a mile you will reach a very sharp left-hand bend, with a track on the right signposted to Biblins. Park a few hundred yards down the dirt track to Biblins and walk the remainder (about three quarters of a mile) to the river. Alternatively if the ferry is operating at Symonds Yat you can start here and complete a circular walk along the banks of the river.

# 74 Whitchurch
## *King Arthur's Cave*

There are a great many caves on the Doward hill near Whitchurch.
King Arthur's Cave is believed to have been inhabited in prehistoric
times, and bones of hyena, cave bear and woolly rhinoceros have
been found in it.

¶While you are in this area it is worth exploring the fascinating
maze of ancient tracks and paths which cover the top of the Great
Doward, especially if you have the 1:25000 map to guide you.

POSITION: Next to a public footpath on the south-western flank
of the Great Doward.
▷ Ordnance Map (1:50000). Gloucester and Forest of Dean 162.
▷ Ordnance Map (1:25000). Monmouth. Pathfinder 1087 (SO 41/
51).
MAP REFERENCE: 546156.

ACCESS: Follow the directions given for Biblins in the previous
entry; you will turn left at the Doward Hotel and then right at the
next 'T' junction. After about half a mile you will enter woodland
and should notice a parking area on the right-hand side of the road
(just *before* the sharp left-hand bend with the turning to Biblins).
Park on this area and walk down the track which leads off on the
right of the road ahead (not the dirt road to Biblins). You will pass
a ruined concrete quarry building and then emerge into a quarry.
The path bears right out of the quarry, with limestone crags on
your left and open fields visible on your right, beyond the edge of
the wood. As you walk down the path, the crags become higher
until you reach the large entrance chamber of King Arthur's Cave.
N.B. Take great care if you decide to explore the cave.

## 75 Whitchurch

### Seven Sisters Rocks — The Finest View of The Wye in Herefordshire?

There are many places in the Wye gorge between Kerne Bridge and Chepstow where the valley sides rise as sheer cliffs of Carboniferous Limestone. Such cliffs are found at Seven Sisters Rocks, where you can stand on top of these massive buttresses and admire the tremendous view into the Wye gorge, with the river hundreds of feet below. The best time to go is late on a summer evening; you may feel a little giddy at the exposed situation, but the atmosphere of the place is unforgettable. *This is not a place to take small children or vertigo sufferers.*

POSITION: On the south-west flank of the Great Doward, about nine miles south-west of Ross-on-Wye.
▷ Ordnance Map (1:50000). Gloucester and Forest of Dean 162.
▷ Ordnance Map (1:25000). Monmouth. Pathfinder 1087 (SO 41/51).
MAP REFERENCE: 547153.

ACCESS: Follow the directions to the Biblins parking place given in the preceding entries. There are a variety of paths which lead towards a clear path which runs along the top of Seven Sisters Rocks. You will almost certainly have to use the map at some point, but if you need a definitive start you should walk back down the road towards the Doward Hotel to find a track doubling back on your left after a hundred yards or so. This track has fields on its right and woodland on its left. After a quarter of a mile you pass King Arthur's cave. Beyond this you should start to turn left towards Seven Sisters Rocks.

# 76 Whitney-on-Wye
## *Wooden Toll Bridge*

The present bridge dates from the 1820s and is supported on wooden piers. You may cross the bridge by car or on foot, and a toll is payable on the north bank.

POSITION: On the River Wye about four miles downstream (north) from Hay-on-Wye.
▷ Ordnance Map (1:50000). Presteigne and Hay-on-Wye 148.
▷ Ordnance Map (1:25000). Hay-on-Wye. Pathfinder 1016 (SO 24/34).
MAP REFERENCE: 258474.

ACCESS: Take the B4350 out of Hay towards Hereford and you will reach the bridge in four miles. Alternatively, take the A438 Brecon road out of Hereford, and keep on this road (turning left after Letton). You will see the bridge on the left after about eighteen miles from Hereford.

# 77 Whitney-on-Wye
## *The Abandoned Footbridge*

Hidden in the woods near Whitney church lies a wooden foot-bridge which crosses the course of the Hereford to Hay railway line.

⟂The bridge carried a useful local footpath over a steep-sided cutting, and was kept in use for many years after the closure of the railway; it was declared unsafe some years ago, and you would be unwise to step onto its rotting timbers. The footpath has been diverted to cross the cutting a few yards further west.

POSITION: Just north of Whitney-on-Wye church.
▷ Ordnance Map (1:50000). Presteigne and Hay-on-Wye 148.
▷ Ordnance Map (1:25000). Hay-on-Wye. Pathfinder 1016 (SO 24/34).
MAP REFERENCE: 267476.

ACCESS: Take the A438 Brecon road out of Hereford, remembering to turn left after Letton. About nineteen miles from Hereford you will see Whitney church on the right, and you should turn up the lane leading to it. Park near the church and follow the footpath uphill towards the wood; you reach the cutting and bridge within one hundred metres.

## 78  Wigmore
### *Picturesque Ruin*

Wigmore was for centuries the stronghold of the powerful
Mortimer family. It was pulled down in the Civil War.
❡ It is possible to explore the ruins which have steps leading down,
past the roots of an ancient tree, to a creepy 'dungeon'.

POSITION: To the west of the village of Wigmore, which is on the
A4110 Hereford to Knighton road, about twenty miles from
Hereford.
▷ Ordnance Map (1:50000). Presteigne and Hay-on-Wye 148.
▷ Ordnance Map (1:25000). Tenbury Wells and Mortimers Cross.
Pathfinder 972 (SO 46/56).
MAP REFERENCE: 408692.

ACCESS: Take the A4110 Knighton road out of Hereford and you
will reach Wigmore in about twenty miles. Turn left up the lane
to the church. You may continue up to the castle on foot by following the track which leads from the higher, right-hand branch of the
lane from the church.

# 79 Wigmore
## The Former Bed of a Large Ice-Age Lake

This area (referred to as the Wigmore basin) was once the valley of the River Teme, which flowed south past the site of Aymestry village. The river was later dammed by ice at this site (see Aymestry and Lucton) and the basin began to fill up with meltwater. Eventually a sizeable 'proglacial lake' was formed and sediments began to settle on its bed. It is this level bed which remains today. The lake itself overflowed at a low point in the surrounding hills, and the rush of escaping water is thought to have cut the Downton gorge, along which the River Teme now flows (having doubled back on itself at The Willows). Looking across the flat expanse of the Wigmore basin, it is not very difficult to imagine it as a large, cold lake under a leaden sky.

POSITION: Within the triangle formed by linking the villages of Leintwardine, Burrington and Aymestry.
▷ Ordnance Map (1:50000). Presteigne and Hay-on-Wye 148.
▷ Ordnance Maps (1:25000). Ludlow, and Tenbury Wells and Mortimers Cross. Pathfinders 951 and 972 (SO 46/56 and SO 47/57).
MAP REFERENCE: The centre of the area referred to above lies in grid square 4270.

ACCESS: Several minor roads cross the area and a public right of way runs across it from The Willows at Burrington (map reference 432714) to Wigmore village (map reference 414691). The area is best viewed from an elevated position on its periphery. There are several such positions along the lane between Leintwardine and Burrington. Other good vantage points are Wigmore Castle (see separate entry) and Croft Ambrey hillfort (442668).

# 80 Yarkhill
## *The Skew Bridge*

The Hereford and Gloucester canal was never a great success commercially, but its obscure remains are a testament to the skill of its engineer, Stephen Ballard (1804–1891). The skew bridge over the canal at Monkhide was designed by Ballard in 1839, and he personally supervised its construction. It is obviously convenient for a canal engineer to make local route deviations whenever road and canal meet, in order to achieve simple right angle intersections (and hence simpler bridge construction). Ballard was not given to making such deviations on the Hereford and Gloucester, and he took this to an extreme in the case of Monkhide, where the road crosses the canal at a very oblique angle. This is possibly the 'skewest' canal bridge in Britain.

❡The brickwork under the bridge creates the impression of being inside a giant rifle barrel; a line of bricks may be traced from one corner of the arch to the corner diagonally opposite.

❡The remains of the canal are difficult to find, but David Bick's book *The Hereford and Gloucester Canal* is an authoritative guide. A society of canal enthusiasts was formed in 1983.

POSITION: Just south of the A4103 Hereford Worcester road, about eight miles from Hereford.
▷Ordnance Map (1:50000). Hereford and Leominster 149.
▷Ordnance Map (1:25000). Great Malvern. Pathfinder 1018 (SO 64/74).
MAP REFERENCE: 612440.

ACCESS: The right turn to Monkhide is clearly signposted about eight miles along the A4103 Hereford to Worcester road. The lane crosses the canal twice, and the skew bridge is the first crossing—reached after less than half a mile. You should park just before the bridge and descend to the towpath.

# References

Beesly P. *A Brief History of the Knight Family*.

Bell S. 'Rail link row traces the track of trams.' *Country Quest* March 1986.

Bick D. E. *The Hereford and Gloucester Canal*.

Bick D. E. *The Old Industries of Dean*.

Bradley A. G. *Owen Glyndwr*.

Bulman J. *Jenny Lind*.

Cox M. A. *M. R. James, an Informal Portrait*.

Freeman B. R. *Shire County Guide—Herefordshire*.

Gavin Robinson S. F. *A History and Description of the Parish Church of St Michael and All Angels, Ledbury*.

Graham R. and Clapham A. W. 'The order of Grandmont and its Houses in England' *Archaeologia*, Vol. 75.

Heins N. 'Flashback' *Hereford Times* 1.3.90

Hollins Murray R. *Dinmore Manor*.

Higham C. *The Adventures of Conan Doyle*.

Hutchinson T. (Ed.) *The Poetical Works of Wordsworth*.

Jervis S. 'Whitbourne Hall, Herefordshire' *Country Life* March 20 and 27, 1975.

Johnson A. and Punter S. *Walks and More—a Guide to the Central Welsh Marches*.

Knowles D. *The Monastic Order in England*.

Knowles D. *The Religious Orders in England*.

Leather E. M. *The Folk-lore of Herefordshire*.

Lewis C. A. (Ed.) *The Glaciations of Wales and Adjoining Regions*.

Lovett W. 'Clodock miller's joke misfired and ended in tragedy.' *Hereford Times*.

Pevsner N. *The Buildings of England—Herefordshire*.

Pfaff R. W. *Montague Rhodes James*.

Plomer W. (Ed.) *Kilvert's diary, 1870–1879*.

Royal Commission on Historic Monuments *Herefordshire*.

Schultz G. D. *Jenny Lind, the Swedish Nightingale*.

Whittaker K. *A Short Account of the Church of St Michael, Garway*.

Williams P. *Whitbourne, a Bishop's Manor*.

Wraight I. and Dyer M. *Real Ale and Cider in Herefordshire*.

Anon. *The Churches of Shobdon and their Builders*.

Anon. *The Church of St Margaret in the Parish of St Margaret's, Herefordshire*.

Anon. *St Catherine's Church, Hoarwithy*.

+ THE·SITE·OF·ST·ETHELBERTS·WELL +

*32   St Ethelbert's Well, Hereford*